HUMMINGBIRDS

Scott Weidensaul

PORTLAND HOUSE

New York

This 1989 edition published by Portland House,
a division of dilithium Press, Ltd.
distributed by Crown Publishers, Inc.,
225 Park Avenue South, New York, New York 10003

Printed and bound in Spain

ISBN 0-517-68848-4
hgfedcba

Library of Congress Cataloging-in-Publication Data

Weidensaul, Scott.
    Hummingbirds/Scott Weidensaul.
        p.   cm.
    Includes index.
    ISBN 0-517-68848-4
    1. Hummingbirds.   I. Title.
QL696.A558W45   1989
598.8'99--dc20   89-31475
                                                          CIP

Produced by: Ted Smart
Managing Editor: Elizabeth Loonan
Design by: Sara Cooper
Editor: Madelyn Larsen
Production Coordinator: Ann-Louise Lipman
Photo Research by: Edward Douglas
Editorial Assistance by: Seni Glaister

For rights information about the photographs in
this book please contact:

The Image Bank
111 Fifth Avenue, New York, N.Y. 10003

HUMMINGBIRDS

When the subject is hummingbirds, superlatives comes easily: brightest, smallest, fleetest. In fact, a hummingbird itself is a superlative, a minute, finely crafted creature no bigger (in most cases) than one's thumb, living life at a ferocious clip, agile beyond compare, with colors that border on garish artificiality. So small and fast are they that it is hard not to think of them as gorgeous insects.

Size notwithstanding, they are birds, merely modifications of the basic avian plan - two wings, a beak, two feet and feathers. Some birds, using the same fundamentals, have developed webbed feet and waterproof feathers for swimming; others, like woodpeckers, are living drills, with padded skulls and chiseled beaks for splitting wood. In each case, form follows function. A hummingbird's "function" is to hover beside flowers and sip the nectar they contain. The evolutionary result is pure magic.

Consider, for example, a tropical species, the Violet-tailed Sylph (*Aglaiocercus coelestis*) of Ecuador and surrounding countries. The male is 8 inches long - but that figure is deceiving, for half of its length is tail, a forked shinglework of sublime beauty, vivid violet-blue that merges seamlessly with iridescent green back feathers. Overlapping the rump are its two wings, enormously elongated and curved, powered by massive (for its size) chest muscles that allow it to move with speed and grace.

In the forests of northeastern South America, the Crimson Topaz (*Topaza pella*) flits high above the dimly lit ground, in the jungle canopy where sunlight flickers through the upper branches of tall trees. The male is as fiery as the Violet-tailed Sylph's colors are cool, with his orange wings and tail, a shining gold throat gorget and a body covered in iridescent crimson. Two of the central tail feathers grow long, curving over each other like crossed military sabers. The bill is long and thin, although not as long as in some hummingbirds. The Sword-billed Hummingbird (*Ensifera ensifera*), for instance, sports a beak that is almost as long as its body and tail combined.

Hummingbirds are a strictly New World family, sprung from the tropical rain forests of South America but now spread across the Caribbean, Central America and through North America as far as southern Alaska and Canada. Most are small, although one Andean species is almost as big as a starling. The tiniest, the Bee Hummingbird (*Mellisuga helenae*) of Cuba, is 2 1/4 inches long, the smallest bird in the world, weighing less than two grams. The standard comparison is to relate the Bee Hummingbird to the Ostrich, which weighs 300 pounds, but the hummer is tiny by any yardstick; a chickadee weighing just a third of an ounce has it outweighed more than four-to-one.

In all, more than 320 species are known. The figure cannot be precise, because new hummingbirds are still being discovered, particularly in the high cloud forests of the Andes.

Structure

For all their beauty, the most remarkable things about hummingbirds are hidden from view.

For a warm-blooded animal, small size presents some substantial problems. Because a hummingbird's body is tiny but its surface area, in comparison, is much greater, it must metabolize energy at an insane pace in order to keep its body temperature at a constant level of about 103 degrees. A larger animal, with proportionately less surface area to lose heat, can live with a slower metabolism and still maintain a high body temperature. This is also why animals living in cold regions tend to be larger and shorter-limbed than relatives that live in warm areas, as with the difference between the big, 200-pound White-tailed Deer of the northern forests and the diminutive Key Deer of Florida that are scarcely larger than a dog. It also explains why hummingbirds face such a tough physiological challenge in just staying alive. They have pushed warm-blooded miniaturization to the limit; any further reduction in size from that of a tiny hummingbird, or the equally small Least Shrew (a mammal) would require more food than could be eaten. The hummingbird has stopped just short of this biological point of no return.

To fuel this internal fire, a hummingbird needs lots of food and lots of oxygen. Research indicates that hummers use up to eight times the oxygen needed by larger songbirds; for this reason, their air passages and lungs are proportionately bigger. A hummingbird's heart is outsized, too. In a large snake - cold-blooded, with extremely low metabolic demands - the heart comprises roughly 0.31 percent of the body mass and pumps at about 20 beats per minute. In a Common Crow, with a higher metabolic rate than the snake, the heart is nearly 1 percent of body weight and beats 340 times a minute. However, in a hummingbird, the heart makes up nearly 2 1/2 percent of the entire body mass and in some species pumps at an incredible 1,200 beats per minute. Compare that with the tinamous, pokey ground-dwelling birds that share many tropical habitats with hummers. Feeble fliers with poorly developed circulation, tinamous have hearts only .2 percent their mass. They live at a far different pace than hummingbirds.

The hummer's blood supply (with enlarged red corpuscles for oxygen-carrying efficiency), feeds the muscles of the chest, which may make up more than a fourth of the bird's total mass. Unlike most birds, in which the power stroke is the downward flap, hummingbirds must be able to exert power on both the up and down strokes in order to hover and fly backwards. At more than 50 beats per second, such flight obviously puts tremendous demands on the bird's muscles.

Every hummingbird known feeds on flower nectar and tiny insects. Nectar is rich in carbohydrates, the insects in protein, but the hummingbird must nevertheless eat incessantly to keep pace with the demands of its body; the nectar is absorbed almost immediately into the blood stream and insects may be digested in as little as 10 minutes.

That is not to say that the hummingbird must feed every minute of every day, only that it cannot regulate feeding to morning and evening, as so many animals do. Studies with Rufous Hummingbirds revealed that they feed in spurts, about 15 per hour, with short periods of restful perching in between. Why? Because each time they feed they fill their crop, then retire, temporarily satiated, while their stomach begins to digest the meal. When the crop is half-emptied a few minutes later, they go out for a refill. Constant feeding is not only unnecessary for the hummingbird, it is impossible. They can feed no faster than their stomach can process the food.

Hummingbirds also carefully adjust their territory size to their feeding demands. On their northward migration, Rufous Hummingbirds rest for days or weeks at a time before moving on. During these layovers, the males set up feeding territories, which they defend against insects and other hummers. Researchers discovered that the hummingbirds fed at the edge of their territory early in the day, when the nectar supply was richest, then retired to the more easily defended center of the territory for the rest of the day, so that interlopers along the territorial edge would find only slim pickings. The biologists also discovered that the hummingbirds determined the optimum size of their territory by trial and error. If the territory was too big, they expended too much energy in defense. If it was too small, there wasn't enough nectar to allow for healthy weight gain before the next hop in the migration.

To reach the nectar, which is stored at the base of the flower's tubular corolla, most hummingbirds have evolved long, thin bills that can probe far into the blossom. The bill itself, however, plays no great role in the act of sipping; it merely serves as a sheath for the hummingbird's remarkable tongue, which does the actual drinking.

Controversy raged for years over just how the hummingbird drinks nectar. The earliest naturalists believed the bill acted as a hollow straw, overlooking the fact that, in many cases, the flower's corolla was longer than the bird's beak. Later observers realized that a feeding hummingbird flicks its tongue rapidly in and out, and speculated that the tongue, not the beak, was the straw. Others noted that the tongue is forked and grooved and, at the tips, covered with fine, fleshy bristles, and so concluded that nectar was drawn up the tongue by capillary action.

It wasn't until recently that the mystery was solved. The tongue is dipped into the nectar reservoir, withdrawn into the bill, then forced out again through the slightly open beak. The outward pressure wrings the nectar from the grooved tongue and it is swallowed as the hummer laps up another load.

The average hummingbird's tongue is substantially longer than the beak that covers it, wrapping back around the skull in another fork and anchoring on the forehead between the eyes - much the same arrangement, incidentally, as is found in woodpeckers, which use their long, barbed tongues as insect spears.

Nectar is not the only liquid food that hummingbirds take. In many parts of North America, sapsuckers drill feeding "wells" into the bark of trees, causing sweet sap to flow. In the Rocky Mountains, Red-naped Sapsuckers have been observed drilling wells in thick clumps of shrubby willows by cutting away sections of bark, creating wide, bare areas that leached sap. Sapsuckers defend such wells against other birds, but when the owner is away foraging at other wells, hummingbirds, like the Rufous and Broad-tailed, are able to flit in for a quick drink. Because they lack the sapsucker's strong, chiseled beak, the hummingbirds would not ordinarily be able to enjoy the sap without this bit of larceny. The hummingbirds are low in the pecking order at the wells; not only do the sapsuckers chase them, but so do red squirrels and warblers that also pilfer the sap. In other parts of the country, Ruby-throated Hummingbirds visit wells drilled by Yellow-bellied Sapsuckers and Downy Woodpeckers.

Conversion to a largely liquid diet has, as might be expected, changed the hummingbird's digestive plumbing as well. The gizzard, the muscular chamber that in other birds crushes hard seeds and nuts, is greatly reduced in size. Absent completely is the caeca, an intestinal dead-end that in some birds, like grouse, may be as long as the small intestine itself, and which digests the fibrous foods that are not part of a hummingbird's diet.

Cellulose in plant leaves and stems is difficult to digest, explaining why intestines are very long in herbivorous birds (up to 46 feet in Ostriches). By contrast, a hummingbird's, geared for absorption of nectar, may be as short as 2 inches.

Although nectar is an energy-rich food source, it is nevertheless made up mostly of water. In order to take in enough energy to stay alive, a hummingbird must drink far in excess of what it needs to replace the water lost through normal excretion and respiration and must get rid of that excess without disrupting its body's delicate balance of salts and minerals. Its kidneys are adapted to the daily deluge, however, and each day the hummingbird passes liquid equivalent to nearly 80 percent of its body weight.

There is little variation among hummingbird bills. Most are roughly a third or fourth of the bird's total length, straight or slightly down-curved. That is a broad generalization, however, and there are many exceptions. The most remarkable is the Sword-billed Hummingbird, which has a 4-inch rapier beak as long as its body and tail combined, and which allows it to feed on the tubed flowers of a number of tropical plants - species like the passion flower, with a 4-inch corolla that puts the nectar beyond the reach of other birds and insects.

The White-tipped Sicklebill (*Eutoxeres aquila*) of northern South America has the most severely curved bill of all hummingbirds, a lancing half-circle that it uses to probe the blossoms of heliconia. Unlike most hummers, the Sicklebill perches to feed, clinging to the heliconia's red flowers while it pokes and prods.

It was once thought that each hummingbird's bill corresponded to the shape of a particular flower. That is now known to be false, although those species with longer beaks tend to feed from longer, deeper blossoms, because the competition is less. The Stripe-tailed Hummingbird (*Eupherusa eximia*) of Central America has a small beak - leading one to believe that it feeds on small flowers with shallow corollas. Not so; its uses its sharp beak to drill holes at the base of deeper flowers, thus gaining access to nectar that would ordinarily be out of its reach. The Purple-crowned Fairy (*Heliothryx barroti*) of Central and South America does the same thing, as do several other short-billed species. That is fine for the bird, but often not good for the plant, which may be reliant on hummingbirds for pollination. A Stripe-tailed stealing in the back way won't touch the pollen-bearing anthers up front, perhaps leaving the flower in a reproductive lurch.

The same snatch-and-run technique, incidentally, is used by some of the honeycreepers, a group of tropical birds related to buntings. Known as flower-piercers, they use their hooked upper beak to grip the flower and their sharp lower mandible to punch a tiny hole in the corolla, then lap out the nectar with a bristled tongue very much like a hummingbird's. In such ways does evolution mold the form of a creature, adapting unrelated groups to similar niches through frequently similar means.

Flight

Evolutionary pressures have also greatly modified the hummingbird's wings. In most birds, forward flight is the only kind possible; the bird flaps with a largely vertical "rowing" motion, with the downstroke providing forward motion and lift. The upstroke, in which the wing is partially folded, is merely a passive movement to prepare for the next downward powerstroke.

A hummingbird's flight is different. Because the wings are so small, both upstrokes and downstrokes must generate lift to keep the bird aloft. In forward flight the wings remain fully flexed, although in the upstroke the wing pivots back slightly. It is hovering flight - a hummingbird speciality - that calls for the biggest changes in technique and structure.

The wing bones of a bird correspond roughly to the arm and hand bones of a human. The humerus runs from the shoulder to the "elbow," where it joins the radius and ulna, the two thinner bones of the lower arm. In a person, the radius and ulna conect with the small carpal bones of the wrist, but in a bird, the carpal and metacarpal bones are elongated, tipped with three small phalanges, the "fingers," which to a bird serve as the anchor for the large primary flight feathers.

In a soaring bird like a Red-tailed Hawk, the humerus, radius and ulna are rather long and the shoulder socket allows motion along a generally vertical alignment. A hummingbird is different; the arm bones are quite short and are fused, so that the elbow and wrist have little movement. The carpals and phalanges, however, are long, taking up most of the wing, and the shoulder girdle is unusually flexible, so the wing can move freely on both the horizontal and vertical planes.

Add to these skeletal changes the hummingbird's phenomenally powerful chest muscles. Like swifts and falcons, which also rely on rapid flight, hummingbirds have deep keels, or sternums, that allow the anchoring of muscles that are heavy for the size of the bird; in a Ruby-throated Hummingbird, the flight muscles may make up more than 30 percent of the body weight. Breast muscles come in two forms: elevator muscles which raise the wing and are, even in active fliers, rather small; and depressor muscles, which in most birds do the majority of the work in flight. In hummingbirds, which need power on both strokes, the elevators are still the smaller of the two kinds, but the disparity is narrowed to only one-half the size of the depressors, rather than one-ninth in a robin.

As a result of the unique wing structure and heavy musculature, a hummingbird can flap its wings in ways that are impossible for other birds, allowing it to fly in ways that seem equally impossible. To hover, a hummingbird holds its body almost upright, then flaps horizontally in a shallow figure-eight. As the wings swing back, they tilt almost flat, forcing air upward, then are brought upright for the forward stroke, which drives air down. The net effect is to keep the hummingbird suspended as though hanging from an invisible thread. In terms of muscular energy, hovering is hideously expensive, requiring tremendous exertions, but it makes the hummingbird's life of nectar-sipping possible.

To fly backwards - something that even scientists believed impossible until high-speed photography proved it - a hummingbird's wings reach back, scooping into the air like a swimmer doing the backstroke. At rest, the hummingbird can't fold its wings into a compact package, as can most birds. All it can do is lap the permanently extended wings back over its tail, out of the way. During waking hours, however, the wings are rarely out of use. A hummingbird is so streamlined for a life of flight that its feet are tiny and all but useless for walking, so even a small shift of position calls for a momentary take-off and landing.

Each species has its own pace, but a hummingbird's wingbeat is fairly constant, regardless of the type of flight in which it is engaged. Most hummers average about 50-58 beats per second, and some have been measured at 200 per second in courtship flight - an astounding number, although not surprising when the size of the wing is taken into consideration: the smaller the wing, the faster it can be flapped. Oddly, the martin-sized Giant Hummingbird flaps at a relatively sedate 10 beats per second, slower than many songbirds with bigger wings and more bulk.

Small though they be, an average hummer's wings can move it along at a healthy clip. Ruby-throats in wind tunnels can make headway against winds up to 27 miles per hour (far less than the 60 mph often cited for free-flying birds, probably achieved with the help of tail winds). Some tropical species have been timed in wind-tunnels at much faster speeds, exceeding 45 mph. Because of their small size and agility, hummingbirds usually seem to be moving faster than they actually are, as they swarm around a feeder or buzz overhead in a mountain meadow, those impossibly small wings a blur against the sky.

Actually, in relation to its body size, a hummingbird has a surfeit of wing area, when compared to a larger bird like a Canada Goose. A Ruby-throated Hummingbird, for example, weighs 3 grams and has a wing surface area of about 12.5 square centimeters. The goose weighs roughly 11,600 grams, and has a wing area of 6,800 square centimeters. The hummer, in other words, has 4.2 square centimeters of wing area for every gram of body weight, while the goose has only .6 per gram. Such a measurement is known as wing-loading and shows that flight is a problem at the upper end of the scale, not the lower.

Small size and agility makes it difficult for predators to catch hummingbirds and may explain the group's legendary cockiness in the face of danger. Hawks, which share the inland mountain ridges of the East each fall with migrating Ruby-throats, may be harassed mercilessly by their fellow migrants. In the breeding season, such attacks play an obvious role in defending the nest, but occasionally the hummingbird is the victim. Those rare times that hummingbirds have been seen to be caught, the predator was usually a falcon or an accipiter, the fastest and most agile of hawks. Others have been known to fall victims to large songbirds like orioles, to frogs, fish and occasionally to tree-climbing snakes Dragonflies and praying mantises occasionally catch them instead of the insects they normally eat. The webs of large spiders, like the Black-and-yellow Argiope of the East, sometimes ensnare hummers.

Metabolism

Anyone who has ever held a small bird in the hand, and felt the rapid pulse of the heart and lungs, realizes that these tiny creatures live life on a faster clock than humans. Yet, compared to hummingbirds, even a chickadee is a sloth.

Metabolism is the chemical and physical process that keep an animal alive: the transfer and use of energy, the creation of heat, all the bodily functions that keep tissues functioning. A standard method of measuring the metabolism of a warm-blooded animal is to calculate its body heat production in calories, per kilogram of body weight. That measurement, taken at rest and extended over a 24-hour period, is considered the metabolic rate and while it may not be strictly accurate (no bird, for example, is going to remain quiescent for 24 hours), it does lend itself to useful comparisons. A chicken, for example, has a resting metabolic rate of 50 calories, while a wren's caloric output is nearly 600. But a hummingbird - at rest, not in active flight - has a metabolic rate exceeding 1,400 calories.

A hummingbird can keep even with its body's demands during the day because it can feed whenever it needs to. But hummers don't fly at night, so they must conserve energy until the sun rises again. In the tropics, where night-time temperatures are fairly high, the hummingbird can simply perch quietly. However, energy conservation becomes an especially sticky problem in mountains and deserts, where the temperature drops at night. To maintain a high metabolism in such cold conditions would actually call for an increase in food.

Many hummingbirds have adapted by borrowing a trick from mammals. They go into a torpor, similar to hibernation, that lasts through the night. Measurements on Blue-throated Hummingbirds (*Lampornis clemenciae*), for instance, showed that at an air temperature in the 90's, the bird's heartbeat would range between 480 and 1,200 per minute, but drops to only 36 per minute at night, when the air temperature is around 60 degrees. In many of the hummingbirds tested, body temperatures would likewise sag into the 50's or 60's, roughly half of its normal level.

While many hummingbirds are known to become torpid at night, a study done on Anna's Hummingbird (*Calypte anna*) revealed that incubating females of that species were somehow able to keep their body temperature high all night without starving, thus protecting their eggs from a chill. In Wyoming's Rocky Mountains, female Calliope Hummingbirds (*Stellula calliope*), were found to remain metabolically active through the cold mountain nights because their thick nests provided adequate insulation against the cold, apparently the same reason that the Anna's Hummingbirds can stay active, too.

The ability to become torpid is by no means restricted to North American species. Many of the high-altitude Andean hummingbirds rely on the same trick to live through the bitter nights on the mountain slopes. Torpidity is still not fully understood, although it seems that it is an emergency measure used only when food supplies have grown scarce. In areas where flowers (or artificial feeding stations) are abundant, hummingbirds may maintain a daytime metabolism through the night, thus avoiding the danger that comes from being unconscious should a predator threaten. Waking from a torpor also requires a substantial energy investment - one that a severely stressed hummingbird may find impossible to make.

Hummingbirds are not the only birds to exhibit such temporary torpors; the swifts (to which hummingbirds are believed to be related) can also become torpid, although usually it happens only when bad weather and a lack of food force them to the edge physiologically. The Poor-will, a relative of the nighthawk, is known to hibernate through the winter in the Southwest, but does not slip into a torpor on the regular basis that some hummingbirds can command. Some hawks are known to lower their metabolism in the winter as a way of reducing food consumption in response to scarce food supplies.

Just as hummingbirds must be wary of fatal nightime cold, so must they avoid overexertion in hot weather, when the high ambient temperature reduces the dissipation of body heat and makes overheating a real threat. Many hummers, like the Broad-tailed Hummingbird (*Selasphorus platycercus*) of the Rockies, seek out shady groves in the heat of the day. Hummingbirds will also bathe, which has the dual benefit of cooling their body and keeping their plumage in top shape.

Feather Color and Form

The colors of a hummingbird are breathtaking in their spectrum-ranging variety and shimmering intensity. No other group of birds possesses such a riot of iridescence.

The secret lies in the structure of the feathers. Color in nature can come two ways - through pigment, like the red of a tulip blossom, or structurally, by fracturing white sunlight into its component colors. Most birds bear pigmented colors: the brown of a grouse, the brick-orange of a robin's breast or the yellow of a goldfinch. Each color is produced by a specific pigment in the feather; zooxanthin, for example, is the pigment responsible for the brilliant yellow of the goldfinch. White light that strikes a feather pigmented with zooxanthin is absorbed, all except for the yellow, which is reflected back. Our eyes see this reflected color and take it for the "true color" of the bird.

Hummingbirds are different. Much of their color is structural rather than pigmented (although many, like the Rufous Hummingbird (*Selasphorus rufus*), have large areas of pigmented color as well). The iridescent feathers of a hummingbird - usually at least the throat gorget and head on males and the back of both sexes - rely on layers of special cells that cover parts of the feathers. Light that hits these cells is broken apart. Some wavelengths are reinforced and intensified, while others are nullified through spectral interference. The resulting colors are amazingly vivid, but unlike pigmented colors, can be seen only when light is hitting the feathers at precisely the right angle. Thus, a hummingbird can shift its position fractionally, and what had been a flaming gorget of red will suddenly quench and go black.

Slight changes in feather structure, angle and the distance between the interference cells can produce a kaleidoscope of colors, and it seems that hummingbirds as a group display almost every one conceivable. Reds, oranges and golds are common, as are blues and violets. The most common iridescent color is green, found on the bodies and backs of many species; because the barbules of the back feathers are curved, rather than flat as in the gorget, the color can be seen from almost every angle.

None of this explains why a hummingbird is cloaked in such royal fashion. The colors obviously play a significant role in courtship. But why this extravagance of iridescence, rather than the pigmented colors that serve for the vast majority of birds? The answer is unknown - although perhaps the better question is: Why not?

Just as a mammal is not covered uniformly with fur, neither is a bird covered at random with feathers. In almost all birds they grow in tracts, sprouting in neatly ordered rows, then blossoming up and out to shingle the bird completely.

Hummingbirds are no different. There are eight major tracts on an average hummingbird, as with most small birds: the capital tract on the head; the humeral on the leading edge and upper surface of the wing; the alar, comprised of the primary and secondary flight feathers; the ventral, paired tracts on the belly; the spinal running down the neck to the tail; the femoral on the flanks; the crural, which is scattered across the legs; and the caudal, made up of the tail feathers. Even within the tracts, there is unexpected order, with feathers arranged in rows. Ordinarily, the belly is more sparsely feathered than the back - in part, because the female needs to expose her eggs to heat-generating skin, rather than the insulating feathers. What seems random to the eye is precisely plotted and with good reason, for a bird's life depends on its feathers, a hummingbird's no less than an eagle's.

In their enthusiasm for learning the minutiae of bird biology, scientists have laboriously plucked many species of birds, painstakingly counting every feather, from the largest primary to the smallest bit of down. It will come as no surprise that hummingbirds have the fewest feathers on a per-bird basis - about 1,000 for a Ruby-throated hummingbird, compared to more than 25,000 for a Tundra Swan. But that figure - like the small size of a hummingbird's wing - is misleading. For its size, the hummingbird has far more feathers than larger birds - 300 per gram of body weight versus only 4 per gram for the swan. The same holds true for surface area; a hummingbird has one-tenth the skin area of a Brown Thrasher, but only one-half the number of feathers.

North America's 13 breeding species of hummingbirds, although not as spectacular as many of the tropical species, are nonetheless beautiful. The two most widespread are the Ruby-throated Hummingbird of the East, (*Archilochus colubris*), and its western relative the Black-chinned Hummingbird, (*Archilochus alexandri*). The two are very similar - in fact, the females cannot safely be differentiated in the field. The male Ruby-throat sports a bright crimson throat gorget, while the Black-chinned has a black gorget with a band of violet on its lower third. The females have white throats and both sexes have iridescent green heads and backs.

The American West, particularly the Southwest, has the greatest diversity of hummingbirds in the country. Canada, on the other hand, has a sparse showing - the Ruby-throat from the prairie provinces east and in parts of British Columbia the Black-chinned, the Rufous, Anna's and the Calliope Hummingbird, the smallest bird in North America.

The Calliope is just 3 1/4 inches long, with a streaked gorget of purplish-red on the male. The Anna's, on the other hand, has a throat and head completely covered with rose-red iridescence, making it one of the most attractive of North American hummingbirds. The male Rufous has a copper gorget, green head and an orange body, save for its white chest and belly. Closely related to the Rufous, the Allen's Hummingbird (*Selasphorus sasin*) has a green back instead of orange and is found only in a narrow band of Pacific coast, mostly in California.

The Broad-tailed Hummingbird looks superficially like a clone of the Ruby-throated, with a red gorget and green back on the male; fortunately, the range of these two species does not overlap, the Broad-tailed being restricted to the western mountains. Costa's Hummingbird (*Calypte costae*) of the desert Southwest is almost as tiny as the Calliope; the male has a unique gorget of purple that flares out to either side like a long mustache, and merges with a similarly colored helmet.

The mountains of extreme southeastern Arizona and southwestern New Mexico, hard astride the Mexican border and of the Big Bend region of Texas, harbor a number of Middle American species that reach their very northern limits there. Their plumage and colors are somewhat more exotic than the other, wider-ranging hummingbirds of the U.S. and Canada. For example, the Magnificent Hummingbird (*Eugenes fulgens*), fomerly known as Rivoli's Hummingbird, has a lime-green throat, purple cap and bright green body; at 5 1/4 inches, it is also the biggest U.S. hummer. Only slightly smaller is the Blue-throated Hummingbird - actually one of the dullest of our native hummingbirds, with a gray body, green back and, on the male, a small blue gorget. The Blue-throat's unusually large, dark-blue tail, marked with prominent white corners, is its most striking feature.

Other border specialities include the Broad-billed Hummingbird (*Cynanthus latirostris*), with a rich, blue gorget and red, black-tipped bill; the Violet-crowned Hummingbird (*Amazilia violiceps*), which matches a purple head and a pure white throat with no gorget patch; and the Lucifer Hummingbird (*Calothorax lucifer*), a purple-throated species that has a distinctly down-curved beak. The colors given are for males; only the Violet-crowned has sexes that are similar.

Through Central and South America - the stronghold of the hummingbird family - the combination of colors and shapes runs riot. Males of many species carry outlandishly long tail feathers. The Red-tailed Comet (*Sappho sparganura*) of the Andes carries a forked tail of gold-tinged crimson, each overlapping feather tipped with black. On Jamaica, the Streamertail (*Trochilus polytmus*) is a common bird, trailing behind it delicately tapered tail feathers that cross like an ethereal pair of scissors. In the Racquet-tailed Hummingbird (*Ocreatus underwoodii*), the central tail feathers of the male are long, but the shafts are bare, save for flattened disks of dark blue at the tips - an adornment shared by a number of other species, including one known as the Marvelous Spatuletail (*Loddigesia mirabilis*), in which the long quills cross, then flare far out to either side. The Black-tailed Train-bearer (*Lesbia victoriae*) of the eastern Andes reaches a length of up to 10 inches, 6 of which are tail. At times, a hummingbird's tail can be so spectacular that the rest of the bird seems to be an afterthought.

Tails need not be long to be beautiful. *Coeligena torquata*, the Collared Inca of the Andes, has a fan-shaped tail of white, with a black band down the middle and heavy black edging. A similar color scheme appears in the Velvet-purple Coronet (*Boissonneaua jardini*) of Bolivia and the Black Jacobin (*Melantrochilus fuscus*) of Brazil, which has no iridescence but is handsome in black and white alone.

Such beauty is not limited to the tail. Quite a few hummingbirds, especially the group known as coquettes, have crests; the Tufted Coquette (*Lophornis ornata*) of South America has a green face, an orange crest amd spotted cheek patches that jut back like rambunctious sideburns. In the Adorable Coquette (*Lophornis adorabilis*), the crest is white and red and the cheek patches are green. The Bearded Helmetcrest (*Oxypogon guerinii*) of the high mountains of Columbia and Venezuela has a triangular black facial patch that tapers, at one end, into a long crest and at the other into a "beard" that droops down over the chest.

Through all this exuberance of masculine color, the females get lost in the shuffle - which is the way nature intended it to be. Female hummers tend (with some exceptions) to be much plainer than their mates, but that makes sense when one considers that the females need no bright courtship plumage. In fact, colors - even those of such a fickle nature as iridescence - would be a hazard as a female sits motionless on the nest through the long incubation, prey for passing predators, robbed of the agility a hummingbird enjoys on the wing.

Neither is every male hummingbird a colorful creature. Their photos rarely grace books, but many species are rather drab. The largest of all hummers, the Giant Hummingbird (*Patagona gigas*) of the Andes, is one of these; were it not for its great size, this plain brownish bird would elicit little or no comment. The genus *Phaethornis*, the hermits of South America, are almost all dull-colored, as evidenced by many of their common names: Scale-throated, Pale-bellied, Gray-chinned, Dusky-throated and Sooty-capped.

Evolution

Humans categorize everything, including living creatures. We lump and group, attempting to force order upon a chaotic world.

A family tree drawn for the living species of birds, for example, has a deceiving neatness about it; each family is carefully placed among its relatives, from the primitive loons and grebes on through the (presumably) more recent perching birds.

But birds make poor fossils - their thin, hollow bones are frail and decompose easily, so the fossil record that shows their genealogy is sparse, and relationships between the various families are often little more than educated guesses.

Hummingbirds were once thought to be related to swifts, part of the same general branch as nightjars and oilbirds. None of these birds look the least bit like hummingbirds; swifts have long, curved wings, but have tiny bills, while nightjars like the Whip-poor-will, are night-flying insect eaters with enormously wide mouths and long, graceful wings. They are all considerably larger than hummingbirds.

Still other authorities place hummingbirds and swifts closer to the woodpeckers, barbets and honey-guides. In recent years, hummingbirds have been placed in their own order, *Trochiliformes*, seperate from other birds, which simply begs the question. Obviously, the jury is still out, and likely to remain so for quite a while.

As the differences between swifts and hummingbirds illustrates, relationships between groups of living things cannot always be surmised based on physical appearances. Hummingbirds and swifts share such internal features as the same number of ribs and an unnotched posterior sternum. Both have short legs almost useless for walking and there are striking similarities in the structure of the wings.

But what of the bill - so long in the hummingbird, so short in its supposed cousin? As a glance through a field guide will show, beaks are (evolutionarily speaking) one of the most pliable parts of a bird's anatomy, easily molded by natural selection to fit a particular lifestyle. Even within families, there are wide differences - the family *Scolopacidae*, the sandpipers, boasts beaks of every size, from the Long-billed Curlew's extravagant, drooping bill, to the short, straight beak of the Spotted Sandpiper. Among hummingbirds the variety is as great: the Sword-billed Hummingbird's four-inch beak, the tiny poker of the thornbills, the curved beak of the White-tipped Sicklebill and the oddly shaped beak of the Mountain Avocetbill, (*Opisthoprora euryptera*) of Ecuador and Bolivia, which points upward.

Unlike many, presumably older groups of birds, hummingbirds are remarkably flexible in their adaptability and appear to be undergoing rapid evolution. The creation of the Andes some 25 million years ago was instrumental in the wide speciation of hummingbirds, for the upthrusting mountains cut off populations from each other, isolating them in fertile valleys bounded by cold, arid peaks.

Like other groups of birds that are also rapidly evolving new species - ducks and wood warblers, for example - hummingbirds are prone to hybridization, because many species are very closely related, having only broken off from each other in the very recent past. The longer a species exists, developing in its own unique direction, the smaller the chance for hybridization, should geographic barriers break down.

Exactly what the hummingbird's ancestors were and what they looked like, can only be guessed at. However, it is reasonable to suppose that the ancestral hummingbird was lured to flowers first by the insects they attract, much as orioles in North America feed on nectar as a supplement to their insectivorous diet; perhaps in the course of time, orioles, too, will evolve specialized body parts or behavior that will allow them to use nectar as a major food source, rather than merely a sidelight. So it must have been for ancestral hummers. Discovering the rich store of food that the nectar represents, those individuals with somewhat longer bills and tongues prospered, passing on those traits to their offspring. It has been suggested that hummingbirds, because the males are polygamous (and thus pass on their genes to a large number of offspring by many females), are excellent candidates for rapid evolution. It is also clear that the ancestral stock originally lived in the Neotropics, where hummingbirds are still most abundant, and only later spread up into North America and south to Tierra del Fuego.

Nectar is an excellent food and it is not surprising that hummingbirds are not the only birds to have taken advantage of it, although they are alone in their development of hovering flight and overall reduction in size to insectish proportions. In Africa, sunbirds have evolved long bills and specially adapted tongues, much as hummingbirds have. On the Hawaiian islands, the niche is filled by honeycreepers, while in Australia, honey-eaters and lories (small parrots) exploit the food supply. While the honey-eaters have long, curved bills, the lories have the standard parrot beak, short and hooked. Instead, the lories have tongues tipped with a fleshy brush, used for licking nectar from the open (rather than tubular) flowers they frequent. The tongue of a Hawaiian honeycreeper is forked, ending in a fringe and is rolled into a tube for the last half of its length.

As hummingbirds have adapted to flowers, so, too, have some flowers adapted to hummingbirds. In North America, hummingbirds pollinate many species of wildflowers along with insects, but in the tropics, quite a few flowering plants have evolved to cater solely to hummers.

While ancient by human standards, animal pollination of flowers is a fairly recent development. The first forests were full of giant clubmosses and treeferns, which reproduced by spores, in alternating sexual and asexual generations. The spores were scattered by the wind, and even later, more advanced plants like conifers relied on this haphazard method of pollination. Vast quantities of pollen were released into the breeze, in the biological hope that a few wayward grains would be blown onto an egg-bearing cone in another tree.

The amount of pollen required for wind pollination is staggering; many northern lakes become cloudy and yellow each spring from the haze of pine and spruce pollen that settles onto the water. Eventually, a better method developed: the flower.

Without animals, a flower is all but useless. The wide, colored petals provide an advertisement and a landing strip and odor serves as a further enticement. The visiting animal picks up pollen from the anthers, or male organs of the flowers and at its next stop unknowingly brushes some of the pollen off on that flower's stigma, the femal organ. Fertilization occurs, with the investment by the flower of a microscopic fraction of a pine tree's pollen output.

Insects, hummingbirds and other animal pollinators don't perform this service out of altruism, of course. The payoff is nectar, a sweet, sugary liquid that the flower produces solely as a bribe for the animal's visit, which it eats along with some of the pollen.

Each flowering plant has its own set of major pollinators and through selective pressure, flowers have adapted to suit the needs of their particular pollinating creatures. Skunk cabbage, for instance, blooms in very early spring, often before the snow has completely melted. Its globular, fleshy flower is hidden inside a purplish spathe that appears weeks before the large leaves. This early in spring (March, in many areas), butterflies and bees are still inactive. However, flies are excellent pollinators and they stir even on chilly days, so the skunk cabbage attracts them with an odor like that of rotten meat.

Butterfly flowers have their own adaptions - wide areas to allow easy landing (often the flowerlets are arranged in flat umbels) and bright colors, as well as pleasing odors that draw bees. Not surprisingly, hummingbird flowers are finely tuned to the needs of the pollination hosts. Generally speaking, such hummingbird flowers have long corollas, abundant nectar and bear their blossoms away from entangling leaves; many hummingbird flowers droop or hang, making it easy for a hovering hummer to drink. They frequently lack any odor that would attract insects (hummingbirds, like almost all birds, have virtually no sense of smell) and usually have no lip to provide a bee or wasp with a landing place.

When the hummingbird sidles up for a drink and slips its bill into the flower, it will likely brush against the anthers, which deposit pollen on its bill or head. In fact, on many hummingbird flowers the anthers curve out and up from the front of the plant, so the pollen brushes against the hummer's head. When the bird visits the next flower, the tiny pollen grains are rubbed off on the plant's stigma, effecting fertilization.

In some tropical forests, hummingbirds pollinate the vast majority of flowers, although many of these flowers are also capable of insect pollination. Regardless, it is obvious that hummingbirds play a valuable role in preserving the plant life of the forest, just as nectar-eating bats are vital to the well-being of many night-flowering tropical species. Evolutionarily, the most specialized of these plants have cast their lots with hummingbirds and should something happen to the birds, the flowers would go unpollinated and species might well die out.

In nature, the web of interconnections between living things is staggering. Hummingbirds, for example, are critical to the lives of many species of tropical flower mites - minute arachnids that use the birds as transportation from flower to flower. Unknown until recently, the mites feed on nectar and each species is often restricted to a single kind of flower. To move between widely separated colonies of plants - an almost impossible journey for so tiny a creature - the mites hitchhike on hummingbirds, hiding in the bird's nostrils until the hummer stops again at a flower of the host species.

The presence of dozens of mites on the sensitive membrane of the nostril is presumably irritating to the hummingbird, even though the mites do no other harm during this uninvited passage. Each time the bird draws near a flower, its rapid-fire breathing draws in a flood of odor, which the mites can detect, even though the hummer cannot. If the flower is of the wrong species, the mites stay put. If it is the correct host flower, they scramble into action instantly, as the hummingbird will not feed for more than a few seconds and the mite that hesitates is lost.

Hummingbirds are a family still wedded to the tropics; the closer one gets to the Equator, the greater the variety of hummingbird species; as many as a third of them live within 5 degrees of it. Despite this abundance of forms, each hummingbird is adapted to a slightly different ecological niche, avoiding direct competition with its relatives. Many species may inhabit the same forest, but feed at different levels, or on different flowers: some in the canopy layer, others at ground level, some in clearings. Although hummingbirds as a group are most successful in the tropics, they have shown adaptability to a wide range of habitats, from moist jungle clearings to cold mountain slopes.

In North America, the Rufous Hummingbird and Ruby-throat are the northernmost representatives of the group, while in South America, the Green-backed Firecrown (*Sephanoides sephanoides*) has adapted to similarly harsh conditions in Tierra del Fuego at the extreme southern end of the continent. A sub-species of the Firecrown, the Juan Fernandez Hummingbird, occupies the Juan Fernandez archipelago some 400 miles west of the Chilean coast. But wider expanses of ocean have defeated the hummingbird, which cannot cross the Atlantic or Pacific, as larger birds routinely do. Consequently, there are no hummingbirds in the tropical and semitropical forests of Asia and Africa, even though environmental conditions there would be perfect for them.

That is not to say it will never happen; the Rufous Hummingbird has demonstrated an adaptability to cold and, conceivably, if it continues to spread north along the Alaskan coast, it might make the short jump across the icy Bering Strait to Asia. But such range expansions are more common among birds like ducks and sandpipers, with greater endurance and more dietary flexibility.

The high mountain valleys of the Andes have also produced countless species. Isolated by the rugged terrain, they have evolved into a myriad of forms and colors and some, like the Marvelous Spatuletail, are found in only one valley. The Spatuletail was known only from a skin sold in the 1800s to the millinery trade, but was rediscovered in the Peruvian Andes some 40 years later. Another highly localized hummingbird, the Chimborazo Hillstar (*Oreotrochilus chimborazo*) is found year-round only on the high sloped Ecuadorian volcanoes, where it nests in caves just below snowline (and so sometimes avoids having to drop into a torpor). Perhaps the highest-altitude species of all, it lives in the Paramos, the alpine meadows at more than 14,000 feet. The Andean Hillstar (*Oreotrochilus estella*) has adapted to the barren environment at altitudes approaching 15,000 feet by seeking caves for shelter and developing somewhat larger legs so it can look for insects on the ground, a food-gathering technique used by another high-altitude hummingbird, the Bearded Helmetcrest.

Sleeping in caves may be normal for hillstars, but most birds, faced with cold weather, simply fly away. Not surprisingly, hummingbirds as a group rarely migrate, since the great majority live in tropical or subtropical climates. In North America, however, almost all of the 13 breeding species move south ahead of the advancing winter, fitting neatly into what is sometimes known as the "southern home theory": birds that evolved in the south and colonized North America are simply retracing their forebearers' paths each year, paths that reached farther and farther from the tropics as the glaciers retreated and the climate warmed. For example, those Rufous Hummingbirds that live in coastal Alaska have the farthest to go, roughly 3,500 miles to central Mexico.

For years this route was considered impossible. Scientists showed in the lab that a hummingbird simply couldn't store up enough fat reserves to last through a journey of nearly 600 miles over open water, even though the bird adds as much as 50 percent of its body weight in fat beforehand. But like the bumblebee that doesn't know it can't fly and so does, the hummingbirds make this incredible trip twice a year - and the scientists later realised that their calculations of flight speed and caloric output were incorrect.

Even today, some hummingbirds are expanding their range to the north, although the change has less to do with glacial retreat and global warming than it does with a new food supply. In the extreme Southwest, where the mountains of Arizona and New Mexico cross the border into Mexican soil, the recent explosion in the popularity of feeding hummers has encouraged Berylline and Violet-crowned Hummingbirds to nest, where once they were only stray visitors. Likewise, Anna's Hummingbirds have expanded in small numbers east into Texas, in part because of the ready availability of artificial feeders.

Courtship and Breeding

As mentioned previously, a male hummingbird's gorgeous colors and strangely shaped feathers are a way of attracting a mate and holding his territory against rivals. But there is more to hummingbird courtship than just pretty colors.

Many species, especially those that live in open country, have ritualized courtship flights. In North America such flights are rather simple, usually a swinging, pendulous affair performed over the head of the female. The Calliope Hummingbird may choose a clearing in the montane forest for his display; the tiny male starts high above the trees, then swoops low through a shallow arc, peaking at his original height before turning to repeat the move again and again. In the same Rocky Mountain forests, the Broad-tailed Hummingbird traces a giant U that may be 60 feet high. The male Anna's Hummingbird follows a similar course, but sings (if the squeaky notes merit the name) as it flies - and as it does so, it carefully orients itself with the sun, so the rose-red gorget flames to best advantage.

If the female is sufficiently impressed, mating will take place in the male's feeding territory, but that is the end of the male's involvement. Nest-building, incubation and chick-rearing, in virtually all species,are solely the domain of the female, carried out in her own, separately defended, nesting territory.

In the tropics, the flashy feathers of many species lend themselves to spectacular courtship displays. The Marvelous Spatuletail is said to angle its tail so its gracefully curving outer quills, with their wide spot of blue at the tips, arch forward to frame its face. The racquet-tails both dance and use their tail quills and small groups of males may cluster about the same female, each trying to woo her into a brief tryst.

In dense tropical forests where visibility is limited, most birds rely on their voice to stake out a territory and attract a mate - birds like the Anvilbird (genus *Procnias*) of Venezuela, which fills the forest with its ringing, metallic cries. Hummingbirds have little vocal ability and although quite a few can sing,their efforts are usually thin and wispy-hardly the ticket for penetrating dense vegetation to advertise one's presence. Many hummers overcome this obstacle by congregrating at traditional courtship sites, very similar to the courting grounds of grouse and some shorebirds. These courtship assemblies of hummingbirds can be rather large; Long-tailed Hermits (*Phaethornis superciliosus*) have been seen in groups of 100 or more. Known as leks (a name applied to any bird mating ground), these groups of displaying or efforts in one well-known spot they increase the chance that a receptive female will see them and allow herself to be mated.

Even in the tropics, flight is an important part of courtship ritual, although the spectacular dives of open-land hummers are largely absent. The Reddish Hermit (*Phaethornis ruber*), which occupies much of eastern South America, is a small, plain hummingbird without iridescence or bright colors; the male is reddish-brown, with a white eyestripe and a simple, tapered tail. But during courtship flight he repeatedly circles the perched female, all the while allowing his long, pure white tongue to hang from his bill. The action may seem bizarre, but it works in wooing the female.

Not all hermits are so particular in their choice of mates. Males of four species have been seen to 'false mate" with leaves, after going through the entire courtship display. It may be that this behavior is a form of displacement activity by frustrated birds, or a type of play-acting by young males in their first mating season.

A hummingbird's song may lack the clear melodic qualities of a songbird's but it fills its purpose. Hummer songs are also more complex than was once thought. Analysis of recordings has shown that songs may vary from lek to lek, even among the same species and at times even among individuals at the same lek. It appears that hummingbirds rely on learning and not instinct for their songs, adopting the prevailing variation of the area in which they live. While such learned vocalization is known from many songbirds, it is found in non-passerines only among hummingbirds and parrots.

Some male hummingbirds, like the Broad-tailed of the American West, have special wing feathers that vibrate in flight, producing a trilling or loud buzzing. The Wedge-tailed Saberwing (*Camplyopterus curvipennis*) of the tropics takes that one step further; the male's wings are curved and reinforced, so that as the bird flies around its lek, its wings produce a startling loud roar. This species also happens to be one of the most accomplished singers among the hummingbirds.

Off the lek, hummingbirds can be fiercely territorial, although not always in the manner normal for birds. Robins, for instance, will defend their nesting territory as a pair, with the male singing to define the boundaries and both sexes chasing away others of their species that intrude. Usually, however, birds ignore individuals of other species, so long as the interloper is not a predator.

However, hummingbirds are polygamous - the male mates with a number of females, establishing no firm pair bonds with any of them. Instead of a pair territory, the sexes may stake out separate plots: good feeding and display grounds for the male, a nesting area for the female. In the Lucifer Hummingbird, the male defends his territory only from other males and the female drives away only other females.

Chick-rearing is arduous work even for a pair of birds, so it is remarkable that in hummingbirds as a group, the females raise the babies alone, and that virtually the entire family is in lock-step on that subject, with hundreds of species rarely, if ever, deviating from the pattern. In a group that has shown such adaptability to climates and conditions, one might expect those species living in harsh environments to bend the rule toward monogamy, but such is not the case.

Among Lucifers in the Southwest U.S. and Mexico, the female waits until she has built her nest before she finds a male for mating; in other hummingbirds, the sequence is usually reversed. For their tremendous range and diversity of color, hummingbirds also all build fairly uniform nests that, despite some changes in form and content, are instantly recognizable as hummingbird nests.

The Ruby-throated Hummingbird's is fairly typical - a small cup of plant down and fibers, bound together with cobwebs and caterpillar silk and affixed to the top of a horizontal branch. When the cup is finished, the female will partially shingle the outside with small bits of lichen, probably for camouflage. Similar nests are built by Blue-gray Gnatcatchers and Eastern Wood-Pewees in North America and they are as frustrating for a bird-watcher to find as the nest of the Ruby-throated Hummingbird in the same woods. Among many species, the female must keep an eye for thieves. In Mexico, the White-eared Hummingbird is victimized by the Green Violet-eared Hummingbird (*Colibri thalassinus*), which may completely dismantle the nest of an unwary White-eared.

Many hummingbirds will lay the foundation for the nest, but have the sides only partially completed, when they lay their clutch of two eggs. The reasons are unclear - in virtually every other kind of bird, nest-building is completed well before the eggs come. One theory holds that the female finishes off the nest after egg-laying because her body is under less stress then and she has more energy to devote to gathering materials. In any event, the nest may double in bulk in the two or more weeks of incubation, rising higher and higher until the cup is deep and thick.

Nest location is more varied among hummingbirds than construction. Hermits frequently cement their nests to the sides of leaves, while one, the Sooty-capped Hermit (*Phaethornis augusti*), suspends hers from a thick strand of spider silk, as does the Planalto Hermit (*Phaethornis pretrei*) of Brazil. To balance her lopsided nest, the female Sooty-capped glues mud pellets to a skirt that hangs below the nest to counter-balance it. Two other genuses of hermits, the *Rhamphodon* and *Glaucis* hummingbirds, use thin fern roots to build a fragile nest.

Virtually all hummingbirds lay just two eggs, which - depending on the size of the adult, of course - are about as big as beans; the smallest, laid by the Vervain Hummingbird (*Mellisuga minima*), is only a quarter-inch long. Small size aside, a hummingbird egg is built and functions just as any other bird egg. The shell is a further refinement on the leathery invention of reptiles, hardened with calcium, protected against the desiccating effects of air, enclosing everything the embryo needs for the first two or three weeks of life.

An average bird eggs forms in about 24 hours within the body of the female: the fertilized egg cell and the yolk, which will provide the food for the embryo, are cloaked in a sterile sheathing, then in the thick albumen (the "white" of the egg). As each layer is added, the egg moves further and further down the reproductive tract, until it reaches the uterus, where it will stay for about 20 hours. It is here that that the calcium-rich shell is excreted, pocked with microscopic pores that allow the transfer of oxygen and carbon dioxide. It is here in many birds that pigment cells color the egg - something that does not occur in hummingbirds, which lay plain, white eggs.

The eggs are usually laid a day apart. Field studies on tropical hummingbirds show that most species lay their eggs around sunrise - a typical schedule for many small birds. When the clutch is complete, she begins to incubate.

A female incubates the eggs to keep them warm, for a chill can kill the fragile embryo quickly. She will sit close, rarely stirring and in birds that form pair bonds, the male will frequently bring food to his sitting mate, or take his turn at warming the eggs. Female hummingbirds have no such support, so they just juggle their own feeding requirements with the rapidly cooling eggs back in the nest, as well as the collection of plant down and cobwebs to finish building the nest.

The incubation period allows the tiny, fertilized egg cell to grow into a chick. Cells divide at a frantic pace, following the genetic coding in the nucleus that somehow allows them to grow more and more specialized as the embryo develops. Each cell, from those that form the beak to those destined to be iridescent gorget feathers, contains the genetic blueprint for the entire bird. Over the course of 2 1/2 weeks, as if by magic, each cell sorts out its own place in the overall plan, and the chick is ready to hatch.

Among shorebirds, waterfowl and gamebirds, the chick breaks out of the egg with its eyes open, covered in down and able to walk and feed itself. Hummingbirds, along with most small birds, do not have such precocial young. Instead, the chicks hatch in a helpless state, their sparse down plastered against their wet skin. The neck muscles are so weak that raising its head for food is a struggle and the head wobbles wildly for several days until the muscles strengthen. The eyes are bulbous but closed and will not open until a week or so has passed. Vibrations from the female landing on the nest, and not vision, are the signal for the twin hummingbird chicks to raise their heads and gape for food.

The development period in hummingbirds is long, compared to some songbirds, with 3 1/2 weeks of care in the nest following the 19 or 20 days of incubation. Even that figure is only an average and many species - especially those at high altitudes - have an even longer wait. Occasionally, a female whose eggs have been killed by cold or rain refuses to give up, like the Anna's Hummingbird that incubated her dead eggs for more than three months. Even after successful hatching, the female must continue to brood the chicks for nearly two weeks, because their bodies are unable to control their own temperature. Heat can be as dangerous as cold, and the female hummingbird whose nestlings are exposed to direct, hot sunlight must keep them carefully shaded to avoid over-heating, while she gapes and pants to keep her own body temperature below lethal levels.

Young hummingbirds hatch with a very short beak, which grows rapidly during the nestling stage. The female feeds by regurgitation, shoving her long bill far down the youngster's throat, then pumping up a slurry of half-digested insects and nectar. This routine is repeated two or three times an hour throughout the day, compared to every few minutes among songbirds. As the chicks grow, their bodies are able to regulate internal temperature, so episodes of brooding dwindle and finally cease - and just in time, because as they grow they strain the confines of the nest, eventually stretching the elastic spider silk walls.

The baby hummer's feathers sprout along the major feather tracts - first sheathed in a translucent straw that protects the growing feather's blood supply, then unfurling when the blood supply dries up and the sheath is preened away. The primaries and secondaries on the wings are the last to break fully from the sheathes, but when they do, the chick is almost ready to take to the air. Feeding and preening interrupt increasing amounts of wing exercise as the young develop, so that by the time they leave the nest, they can fly fairly well and are far better than young passerines, which flail almost uselessly for the first few days of freedom.

In many hummingbirds, the female may start building a second nest, progressing through mating and even egg-laying, while still caring for her first brood of nest-bound chicks. Apparently she can manage the demands of double duty, for most of these premature nestings succeed, even though the chicks from the first nest must be guarded and fed for another two or more weeks, before they are fully self-sufficient.

North America's Hummingbirds

Ruby-throated Hummingbird
Archilochus colubris

The only hummer in the eastern United States and Canada, the Ruby-throat is, for most people, the quintessential hummingbird. The male has a bright red gorget above a white crest, a green head and back and greenish-gray sides. The female and immature males are green above and unmarked white below and both sexes are about 3 1/2 inches long.

Ruby-throats are found from Texas and Nebraska east to the Atlantic. In Canada they extend as far west as Alberta and north through the boreal forest, sticking to woodland openings where wildflowers grow in abundance. Although rarely as abundant, on a local scale, as are some of the western species, the Ruby-throated Hummingbird is a fairly common bird over much of its range and is easily lured to gardens with feeders or the proper selection of flowering plants.

Mating occurs shortly after the birds return from Central America. Courtship takes place in a glade or woodland edge, where the male's nuptial flight can be given to best advantage, as he swings back and forth in a shallow arc, buzzing his wings furiously at the bottom of each swing.

As with all hummingbirds, the female alone builds the nest and tends the eggs, despite the belief by John Audubon that the male exhibits "sincerity, fidelity and courage" toward his mate. The nest is a tiny cup of spider silk and plant down, shingled with lichen and placed on a horizontal tree branch where it is almost impossible to see from the ground. Although by no means universal, many Ruby-throat nests are built on branches overhanging water, perhaps for the added security, perhaps also because of the cooling effect of evaporation near flowing water. Starting with a flat platform affixed to the branch, the female builds up the sides to an inward taper, usually needing about a week to finish the job. Site fidelity is fairly common; one homeowner in Pennsylvania enjoyed the presence of a Ruby-throat nest in the same front-yard maple for six years.

The twin eggs take more than two weeks to hatch and the young spend another week in the nest before fledging. They are fortified with frequent feedings of regurgitated nectar and insects from the female, which plunges her beak down their throats, pumping the slurried food into their stomachs; the performance almost hurts to watch, but does not faze the chicks.

Once out of the nest the chicks stay with the female for a time, eventually heading out on their own. Come early fall, September in most of the Northeast, Ruby-throats begin migrating south. Many of them follow the inland mountain ridges or coastlines, echoing the better-known migration of hawks and falcons, but skimming low along the hills, just barely clearing the treetops. Some Ruby-throats follow an overland route to their wintering grounds in Cental America, while others take a far more hazardous path, down to Florida and across the Gulf of Mexico to the Yucatan peninsula, 600 miles to the southwest.

The spring migration in many areas seems to be timed to the blooming cycle of favorite food plants. In Arkansas, for example, it was noted early on that Ruby-throats arrive at about the same time the dwarf buckeye begins to bloom, an important nectar source in early spring.

Even though hummingbirds are not early migrants, rarely arriving in the northern states before mid-May, the weather sometimes plays cruel tricks on them. A late cold snap, especially in the northernmost part of the species' range, can be deadly, although early ornithologist Arthur Cleveland Bent wrote of a May storm in Quebec that dumped six inches of snow and dropped temperatures into the 20s for several days. The hummingbirds survived, however apparently by foraging for aphids and other tiny insects.

Sadly, the Ruby-throated Hummingbird has shown some serious declines in recent years, dwindling in numbers over much of the eastern half of its range. The causes are unclear, but many suspect heavy pesticide use on the hummer's Mexican and Central American wintering grounds.

Black-chinned Hummingbird
Archilochus alexandri

As the Ruby-throat is the common hummingbird of the East, so the Black-chinned Hummingbird is its western counterpart. It is found from Texas and the Rockies into southern British Columbia and west to the Pacific.

Female Black-chinneds and Ruby-throats are impossible to tell apart in the field, and the males are identical in size and proportion. The only real plumage difference is the gorget, which in the Black-chinned is plain black, with a purple border on the lower one-third. This simple adornment is even more fickle than most iridescent patches and is often not visible.

The Black-chinned is a creature of dry country, inhabiting the chaparral and woodlands, usually near water, although in the summer, when lowland flowers have finished blooming, it will move up into the mountains, where the melting snows and cooler temperatures mean fresh blossoms.

Following courtship that includes a pendulum-like display flight punctuated by the male clapping his wings and giving a quiet, warbling call, the female builds a typical hummingbird nest about 10 or 15 feet above the ground in trees - like the Ruby-throat, often over water or dry streambeds, but without the lichen shingling of its eastern relative. Also like the Ruby-throat, the Black-chinned will return to the same location as the previous year's nesting, even to the extent of building her nest on top of the squashed remnants of the previous year's; one nest in California was three layers deep.

As the nest grows in size through the building process, the female sits in the cup, molding it to her body while keeping the outside neat with her bill. As with several other North American hummingbirds, female Black-chinneds have been known to build a second nest and even to begin incubating a second clutch of eggs, before the first brood of chicks has left the nest.

The wintering grounds for the Black-chinned Hummingbird are in Mexico. Apparently, the sexes migrate at different times, with the males arriving first and the females thereafter. Other hummingbirds likewise show sexual segregation on the trip north; small flocks of Ruby-throats that pause at a rich nectar source are invariably of one sex or the other, although it seems that hummingbirds migrate singly more often than in groups.

Costa's Hummingbird
Calypte costae

Twittering madly, a hummingbird buzzes around the perimeter of a blooming ocotillo, chasing away an interloper before settling down on a high twig, where the desert sun sparkles on his violet face.

This is the Costa's Hummingbird, a tiny slip of a creature that is a common sight in the arid country of southern California, Nevada, Arizona and parts of Utah and New Mexico. Only about 3 inches long, it is surpassed only by the Calliope Hummingbird as the smallest North

American bird. Males are green above, with a violet gorget that extend back in a long finger at each side of the face and merges with a full helmet of the same color. The female is gray-green above and white beneath, with a relatively shorter bill than the similar Black-chinned, but field identification is very difficult.

Back from its Mexican wintering grounds in March or early April, Costa's Hummingbird males set up courtship territories, displaying to females in a series of swooping dives, accompanied by a shrill wing whistle that has been likened to a richocheting gunshot. The female is not at all particular about her choice of nest sites and Costa's nests have been recorded from high in oak trees to low in bushes, weeds and cacti, although on the whole they usually pick a spot within 10 feet of the ground and on the outside of the tree or bush where visibility is best.

If flowing water is in the area, the hummingbirds may show a preference for nesting near it. They also display a fondness for feathers, especially dark ones, which are included in the rim and lining of the nest. While many songbirds line their nests with feathers, this habit is not common among hummingbirds, perhaps because the plant down they ordinarily use is just as soft and insulating.

The Costa's Hummingbird does not linger on the breeding grounds; in the northern parts of its range, where it is migratory, the males depart for their Mexican wintering grounds as early as May or June. The females, with young to care for, must delay their departure, but by July most of those have begun to leave as well. Costa's Hummingbirds stay year-round in parts of southern California and Arizona.

The species is named for the Marquis de Beau-Regard, Louis Marie Pantaleon Costa, a 19th century French nobleman renowned for his collection of hummingbirds. Although the Marquis did not discover his namesake hummingbird, the man who did (Adolphe Simon Neboux) named it in his honor for his work on hummingbirds. This practice, of naming new species after powerful and wealthy patrons, was a mixture of sincerity and calculated flattery, for such patrons frequently were a biologist's major source of funding.

Anna's Hummingbird
Calypte anna

A year-round resident in most of its coastal range, the Anna's Hummingbird is also one of the handsomest of the North American species, with males displaying a head and throat of brilliantly pink iridescence.

The Anna's hummer plays on differences in altitude and season to get the most from each year. In the mild lowlands near the coast, it is able to breed in winter, then is free to move into the mountains as the snows melt and flowers reappear in spring, although nesting may occur also through the summer. When cold weather returns, it shifts its range again to the lowlands and repeats the cycle, which is so nomadic that it cannot be called true migration.

Courtship, as with most U.S. hummingbirds, features an aerial display by the male, rather more elaborate than with many species. The male flies high above his prospective mate, then drops into a deep, U-shaped dive, climbing again above her head where he hovers and sings a mix of squeaky notes. At the lowest point in each dive, he gives an explosive *peck*, which may be mistaken for the alarm bark of a ground squirrel.

The "courtship" flight actually fills a number of roles in the male hummingbird's life, some of them unclear. Immatures practice the flight through fall and winter and territorial adults may use it as a threat display against other hummingbird species or, for that matter, birds of totally different orders.

In typical hummingbird fashion, the male's involvement with family life ends with mating. The females are extremely flexible when it comes to picking nest sites, accepting everything from clumps of flowers to high trees as a base for the spider-web and plant-down cup, although the eggs may be laid tenuously on the nest base before the walls are even constructed. A lining of feathers may also be worked into the finished structure, as with the Costa's Hummingbird.

Ornithology owes a great debt to the thousands of amateur scientists who, over the years, have broadened man's understanding of wildlife and animal behaviour. Today, such research is generally considered the realm of specialists, but in the late 1800s, especially in the frontier West, laymen and women meticulously recorded their observations for science. Some of their conclusions have since been proved incorrect, but in many cases, much of what we know about bird biology still rests on their pioneering studies. One patient gentleman in California in the 1890s spent weeks watching the progress of an Anna's Hummingbird nest, from its construction in early April through the fledging of the single chick (the other egg having failed to hatch) in late May.

Like the Black-chinned, the Anna's Hummingbird has been known to start a new nest while still caring for the first. Immature birds resemble the female, with her red-flecked throat, but as they grow, young males begin to show the outline of the full gorget and helmet they will later display so actively.

As with all hummingbirds, the Anna's feeds on a mixture of nectar and tiny insects, the latter often gathered from the webs of unsuspecting spiders - and occasionally the spider itself.

Very occasionally, a hummingbird will exhibit complete or partial albinism - the absence of pigment. There are scattered records of albinism in Anna's, Ruby-throated and Black-chinned Hummingbirds, although it seems likely that this rare condition is found as well in the less common (and therefore less-studied) hummers.

To be considered a complete albino, a bird must have pure white feathers and pink eyes, rather than the brown-pigmented eyes normally found. The condition is the result of a genetic mix-up, in which the enzyme tyrosinase is absent from the cells. Albinism is more common among certain species or groups (albino robins, for example, are frequently reported), although almost every creature may be afflicted. Albinos usually do not live long - their white color foils any natural camouflage they should possess and the vision of pink-eyed individuals is generally weak.

Calliope Hummingbird
Stellula calliope

The tiniest bird north of Mexico, the Calliope Hummingbird weighs less than a tenth of an ounce - but that doesn't stop it from harassing much larger birds that enter its territory, including hawks. The hummingbird rockets out of nowhere, buzzing straight for the head of the intruder, needled beak aiming for the eye. Although it may not strike, the attack is unsettling enough that few birds tarry.

The Calliope is a high country bird, most common in mountain meadows, along cool streams and in openings in the forests of lodgepole pines and aspens. The male has a gorget made up of thin streaks of iridescent red that extends back beyond the edge of the throat; the female has tiny dark spots on her throat, but her small size, short bill and short tail are better field marks when distinguishing her from other female hummingbirds.

An average Calliope Hummingbird weighs about 2.5 grams. Most birds, including large hawks and eagles, are rarely able to lift objects that weigh more than half their own body weight, but one male Calliope was seen to repeatedly pick up a stunned female and lift her several feet into the air before she slipped from his beak.

Found in the breeding season from British Columbia through parts of Colorado, Utah, Nevada and California, the Calliope ranges farther north than any other hummingbird, except for the Rufous. It also lives at high altitudes, up to timberline in some western mountains, where night-time temperatures are frigid. The males react by slipping into a torpor, but nesting females with eggs to keep warm and with a snug nest in which it pass the night, remain metabolically active, then migrate south to Mexico starting in late summer.

Whether for protection from the elements or from predators, the female Calliope almost always nests beneath a concealing branch or screen of foliage. In addition, the nest is often built on a knot, a dangling pine cone or some other protuberance that accentuates its already excellent camouflage. This species has been known to fix up nests from previous years for reuse, a habit that is rare among small birds, and like the Black-chinned will sometimes rebuild on the flattened foundation of a previous year's efforts.

The bird's name, incidentally, refers not to the steam-powered organ, but to the Greek muse of epic poetry -this, for a bird that is almost silent. The genus name, *Stellula*, means "little star," and is much more appropriate.

Broad-tailed Hummingbird
Selasphorus platycercus

Like the Calliope, the Broad-tailed Hummingbird is a creature of the mountains, found most frequently at altitudes of 4,000 to 10,000 feet, lower in the northern part of its range, higher in the Southwest. It is a common sight in alpine meadows, feeding on the wildflowers that in summer wash over open areas like a colorful tide.

The male looks very much like the Ruby-throated Hummingbird of the East, even though the two are not closely related. The Broad-tailed has a red gorget, green head and body, green sides and a white chest; the female shows pale rufous on the sides and is almost identical to the Rufous and Allen's females. In flight and when hovering, both sexes have a very wide tail with white spots at the outer edges and with less red than on the Rufous Hummingbird.

Actually, sound is the best tip-off that a male Broad-tailed is around, because this species has a unique set of slotted outer primary feathers that create an insect-like trill when the bird flies. This field mark fails, however, during the late summer molt, when the sound-producing feathers drop out temporarily. Should the slots be experimentally covered, so the trilling is eliminated, the male hummingbird usually loses its territory or maintains it at much greater effort - rather like a soldier going to war without a weapon. Once the covering is removed and the slots restored to working order, the hummingbird renews his aggressive attacks on intruders.

The Broad-tailed Hummingbird shows a fair degree of fidelity to old nest sites, often returning year after year. The shape and size of the nest, as well as the materials used to build it, can vary greatly between regions; in some areas they will be shingled with lichen, while in others this covering is absent, or replaced with bits of leaves and bark. The nests are usually built close to the ground on horizontal branches, frequently over running water.

By late summer the Broad-tailed hummers begin to retreat from their mountain homes, beginning the long migration back to the highlands of Mexico and Guatemala, where it mingles with resident birds of closely related subspecies.

Life in the wild is full of hazards, and although hummingbirds seem to be able to avoid trouble much of the time (one reason why their reproductive rate is low, compared to other small birds), their lives are often short. But how short? Banding studies are shedding light on the question, with some surprising results. The longest recorded lifespan for a wild North American hummingbird was a Broad-tailed that lived for 11 years, while Ruby-throats have been known to live nine years. These are maximum figures and by no means do all hummers live to such a ripe old age. Interestingly, the longest recorded span for a wild Allen's is less than four years. Because only about 3 percent of all banded birds are ever recovered, the low lifespan is probably a statistical glitch resulting from the limited data base and it seems likely that Allen's Hummingbird lives about as long as its other close relatives.

Rufous Hummingbird
Selasphorus rufus

Like a bit of flame on wings, the Rufous Hummingbird must certainly rank as one of the prettiest birds in North America, cloaked in orange and copper every bit as beautiful as the flowers on which it feeds

The Rufous is 3 3/4 inches long, although such measurements are only the average. Males and females differ somewhat in size and individuals may be bigger or smaller than the norm, regardless of sex, just as in humans. The male has a coppery gorget, metallic green crown and white chest, but the rest of his body is wrapped in warm orange. Some males may show tiny spots of iridescent green on the back, similar to a male Allen's Hummingbird. The female is confusingly like other western female hummingbirds, but has darker rufous sides and more orange on the tail.

This is the long-distance champ among hummingbirds, migrating farther north than any other species - as far as southcentral Alaska and northern British Columbia, where it sticks to the more temperate coast. In fall it makes a migration that can stretch more than 3,500 miles, to the highlands of central Mexico. What makes the accomplishment even more remarkable, aside from the bird's tiny size, is the fact that out of the hundreds of species of hummingbirds, very few migrate at all - much less over such a distance.

The male may be joined in his courtship flight by the female and Rufous Hummingbirds have been observed mating in mid-air in a manner more usual for swifts than for hummers. It must be noted, however, that hummingbirds are rarely seen mating, regardless of the location. Among tropical species that form leks, the female and her chosen mate usually zip off into the vegetation after the courting display is finished.

Most hummingbirds are solitary during the breeding season, but Rufous hummers have been known to nest in loose colonies in groves of coniferous trees, or among thick-hanging vines, with the nests camouflaged to match their surroundings.

A hummingbird's fondness for the color red is well-known and is rather overstated among a number of species, which will visit yellow, orange or white flowers with equal gusto. But the Rufous does seem, like the Ruby-throat, to have an attraction for red, which leads it to explore anything of that color - porch ornaments, outdoor thermometer bulbs, even bandanas and hair ornaments that are being worn at the time. In a number of parts of the country, this curiosity has gotten Ruby-throats and other species into fatal trouble. One brand of electric fence insulator, made of bright red plastic, has been implicated in the deaths of many hummingbirds. The hummer lands on the electric fence then reaches over to probe the insulator with its beak, searching for nectar. This completes the circuit and the hummingbird is electrocuted.

Allen's Hummingbird
Selasphorus sasin

A very close relative of the Rufous Hummingbird, Allen's Hummingbird is confined to the coast of California and extreme southern Oregon.

At first glance, the two species seem identical, until the iridescent green back of the male Allen's is noticed. The females cannot be told apart in the field and during the migration, when both species may be found in the same area, it is hopeless to even try.

In most respects, the life history of the Allen's is also very similar to the Rufous. Females may nest in small colonies, for instance and the males are, like the Rufous, quite belligerent. The display flight is different, however, with the male swinging back and forth through an arc of some 25 feet, squeaking and making a vibrating sound with his tail, followed by a high climb and a dive from nearly 100 feet up. The nest is built by the female over a period of a week or more.

The Allen's Hummingbird winters in northern Mexico and into the very southern portion of California. Adult males head south first, followed by the females of all ages and, finally, the young males, which negotiate the trip to their ancestral wintering grounds without guidance from adults.

Lucifer Hummingbird
Calothorax lucifer

One of the least common of the U.S. hummingbirds, the Lucifer enters the country only in the Chisos Mountains in Texas, where it breeds, and as a nonbreeding visitor to the Chiricahua Mountains of southeast Arizona. It is by no means a rare bird in Mexico, however, where the core of its range lies.

The Lucifer is the only North American hummingbird with a pronounced down curve to the bill, a field mark present in both sexes. The male has a purple gorget that flares like a Costa's, but lacks any purple on the head. Females have cinnamon underparts and a pale white eyestripe.

The nest is built near the ground in a shrub, and the adults feed extensively on and around the flowers of the agave, as well as capturing insects on vegetation and in the webs of spiders. Where it is found with pugnacious Black-chinned hummers, the Lucifer's is often hounded mercilessly away from the best nectar supplies, even though this species is feisty in dealing with others of its own kind.

Berylline Hummingbird
Amazilia beryllina

As beautiful as it is rare in the U.S., the Berylline Hummingbird has bred on a few occasions in the Arizona border country, but the bulk of its range lies to the south, in Mexico and Central America.

Aptly named for the mineral beryl, the male Berylline is covered in intense green, with a grayish belly and chestnut wings and tail that glisten with purple when the light is right. The female is strikingly similar, with more gray on the belly and less intense green plumage.

In Arizona, the Berylline is usually found in forests and woodland clearings and in well-watered canyons. Very little is known of its life history; the nest is usually found in deciduous trees, built of plant down and spider silk with grass blades dangling below like ribbons. The length of incubation and the nestling period, the number of broods each breeding season and other details are largely a mystery.

The Berylline is one of the Southwestern hummingbirds that appear to be extending their range north thanks to the increase in hummingbird feeders.

Buff-bellied Hummingbird
Amazilia yucatanensis

Another Mexican species that strays over the border into the U.S., the Buff-bellied Hummingbird is an uncommon bird in the lower Rio Grande valley of extreme southern Texas.

Relatively large (at more than 4 inches), the male and female Buff-bellied are colored alike - a bright green head, throat and chest, bronzy back and pale buffy underparts that can appear gray. The bill is red and slightly drooping, with a black tip.

In the breeding season, the Buff-bellied hummer is usually found in dry woodlands and chaparral thickets near the coast, as well as better-watered locations like stream drainages and gardens. The female builds her nest within 8 or 10 feet of the ground, often much lower, on drooping branches in shrubs and small trees. Even though this is a fairly big hummingbird, the nest is only about 1 1/2 inches in diameter, smaller than the average nest of the Calliope Hummingbird, which is a substantially smaller bird.

The Buff-bellied is found through lowland Mexico, Belize and parts of Central America.

White-eared Hummingbird
Hylocharis leucotis

Found in small numbers almost every year in canyons of the Chiricahua Mountains in Arizona, the White-eared Hummingbird's range extends far to the south, through Mexico and much of Central America.

Males and females both have a bold white stripe running from over the eye down along the edge of the cheek, but where the male has a green gorget, the female's throat is white, flecked with green disks. The male also has a purple face and crown. Like the Broad-billed Hummingbird, the White-eared has a red bill with a black tip, but the White-eared's is shorter.

Where it is a common breeder, the White-eared Hummingbird is one of the species that may form singing assemblies of males, gathered in loose concentrations and all giving forth a tiny bell-like song. Each assembly may have its own "dialect", a song that is slightly different from other assemblies, even those in the same general area.

Broad-billed Hummingbird
Cynanthus latirostris

In the dry canyons of southeast Arizona, southwest New Mexico and west Texas, the Broad-billed Hummingbird can be found, flitting with its odd jerky flight from flower to flower.

Fairly common in the proper habitat, the Broad-billed is a frequent sight at hummingbird feeders, plunging its red bill (which is not noticeably wider than most hummingbird beaks) into the feeding port for sugar water.

A male Broad-billed is a handsome bird, with a cobalt blue throat and forehead that blends with the deep green of its body. The female is green above and gray below, with a thin, pale eyestripe that resembles that of a White-eared Hummingbird; the Broad-billed's unbarred sides help separate the two.

The shaggy nest is decorated with bits of leaves and bark, rather than the lichens used by many hummingbirds and is very small for the size of the bird - at least in comparison to the nests of northern hummers, which may have need of greater insulation than this inhabitant of the hot Southwest.

Violet-crowned Hummingbird
Amazilia violiceps

A bright red bill, purple cap and an unmarked white throat are the unmistakable field marks of the Violet-crowned Hummingbird, one of the rarities that draw birders to the border mountains of Arizona and New Mexico. The sexes are alike, further simplifying identification.

When breeding has occurred it has been in moist canyons with large sycamores and cottonwoods, with the nest high above the ground on the branch of a tree. In New Mexico the twin eggs are usually laid in July, although this hummingbird is so rare that it is still largely unstudied.

Magnificent Hummingbird
Eugenes fulgens

Fulgens is Latin for "glittering," and is well suited to the Magnificent Hummingbird, a resident of the Arizona-New Mexico mountains and Bing Bend area.

The Magnificent haunts woodlands and canyons above 4,000 feet, nesting on the horizontal branches of high trees. Males can be confused with no other native hummingbird: the gorget is aqua green, the crown purple and the chest blackish green, with a wide, dark tail. The overall effect, especially if the light is poor, is of an exceptionally big all-black hummingbird, and many birders refer to it fondly as "the Black Knight". The female is very much like a female Broad-billed, only quite a bit larger, with a green back and head, gray belly and white eyestripe.

Formerly known as Rivoli's Hummingbird (named for a French nobleman with an interest in American natural history), the Magnificent ranges south through Mexico, to which it returns each fall on migration.

Magnificent Hummingbirds fly with a wingbeat so slow that the wings can often be seen by the naked eye, and will sail briefly with its wings locked and immobile. Very aggressive toward other hummingbirds, the Magnificent will defend its nectar sources, be they in a contiguous territory or scattered along a "trapline" that the bird visits on a regular schedule.

In determining champion size, which is more important - length or weight? If length is the criteria, then the Magnificent is the largest hummingbird north of Mexico, although only by a whisker. If weight is the key, then the Blue-throated Hummingbird wins, 8.4 grams to 7.7, even though it is fractionally shorter than the Magnificent.

Blue-throated Hummingbird
Lampornis clemenciae

Somberly attired, the male Blue-throated Hummingbird possesses a sort of Quaker beauty, covered in gray, but with a dusty blue throat and a broad, white-tipped black tail. At 5 to 5 1/4 inches, males are as large as the Magnificent Hummingbird - and indeed, there is enough individual variation that some Blue-throats are bigger than some Magnificents.

Most often found in high canyons of the border country mountains, the Blue-throated Hummingbird rarely strays from streams and creeks that water the forests of oak, sycamore and maple. The cup of plant fibers and spider silk is built on a thin twig or (since the coming of modern comforts) an electric line; flowers, long-stemmed plants and ferns may also be chosen. With a tenacity born of curiosity, one observer dismantled a used Blue-throated nest to measure the amount of cobwebbing it contained. His estimate: 15,000 *miles* of spider and caterpillar silk. The incubation and nestling periods are long compared to most small birds, but are normal for hummingbirds: 2 1/2 weeks of incubation, then almost four weeks in the nest before the two chicks fledge.

While the females are nesting, the males may range higher up into the mountains, raiding the nectar sources of smaller hummers or fly-catching for insects. Because it is a robust bird, the Blue-throated often takes fairly large spiders and insects, including wasps and bees.

Previous page: With its incomplete, triangular gorget shielded from the sun, this young male Anna's hummer could easily be mistaken for an immature Black-chinned Hummingbird, which shares part of the same range. *This page:* Hummingbirds do not have an instinctive knowledge of which flowers to visit. By using trial and error they learn to recognize the structure, color and taste of favorite blossoms. *Facing page:* A female Anna's Hummingbird resting. The hummer's sickle-shaped wings have been ideally adapted for rapid wing beats by eliminating most of the secondary wing feathers and paring the primaries down to narrow blades.

Facing page: Flower nectar, so rich in carbohydrates, provides the high-energy diet that hummingbirds, like this male Anna's, need to sustain their ferocious metabolic rate. Tiny insects, plucked from the flowers, provide additional nourishment. *This page:* Asleep on a twig, a male Anna's sits with his feathers fluffed for extra insulation against the night's chill. Like many hummingbirds, the Anna's metabolism drops at night to a level approximately one-seventh of that maintained by day. *Overleaf:* The foothills of California, where wildflowers bloom in summer profusion, are a favorite habitat of the Anna's Hummingbird. Because of the mild climate, most Anna's hummers stay throughout the winter instead of migrating. *Inset:* Enthusiasts can attract hummingbirds like this Anna's to their own yards by filling commercial feeders with a solution of 1 part sugar to 5 parts water. This best approximates nature's own sugar concentration of the wildflower nectars preferred by hummingbirds.

Facing page: After feeding her two chicks by regurgitating nectar, a female Anna's Hummingbird flicks her long tongue to clean her beak. A hummingbird's tongue, much longer than the beak, is forked and bristled like a bottlebrush for lapping nectar. *This page:* Sipping at a thistle, this immature male Anna's Hummingbird is just beginning to molt in its iridescent gorget and helmet. The process usually takes two weeks and requires additional energy for the growing feathers. *Overleaf:* A male Anna's Hummingbird. Most hummingbirds have buzzy call notes, but the Anna's is one of the few North American species with an actual song, a series of chirps and metallic notes given by males in the breeding season.

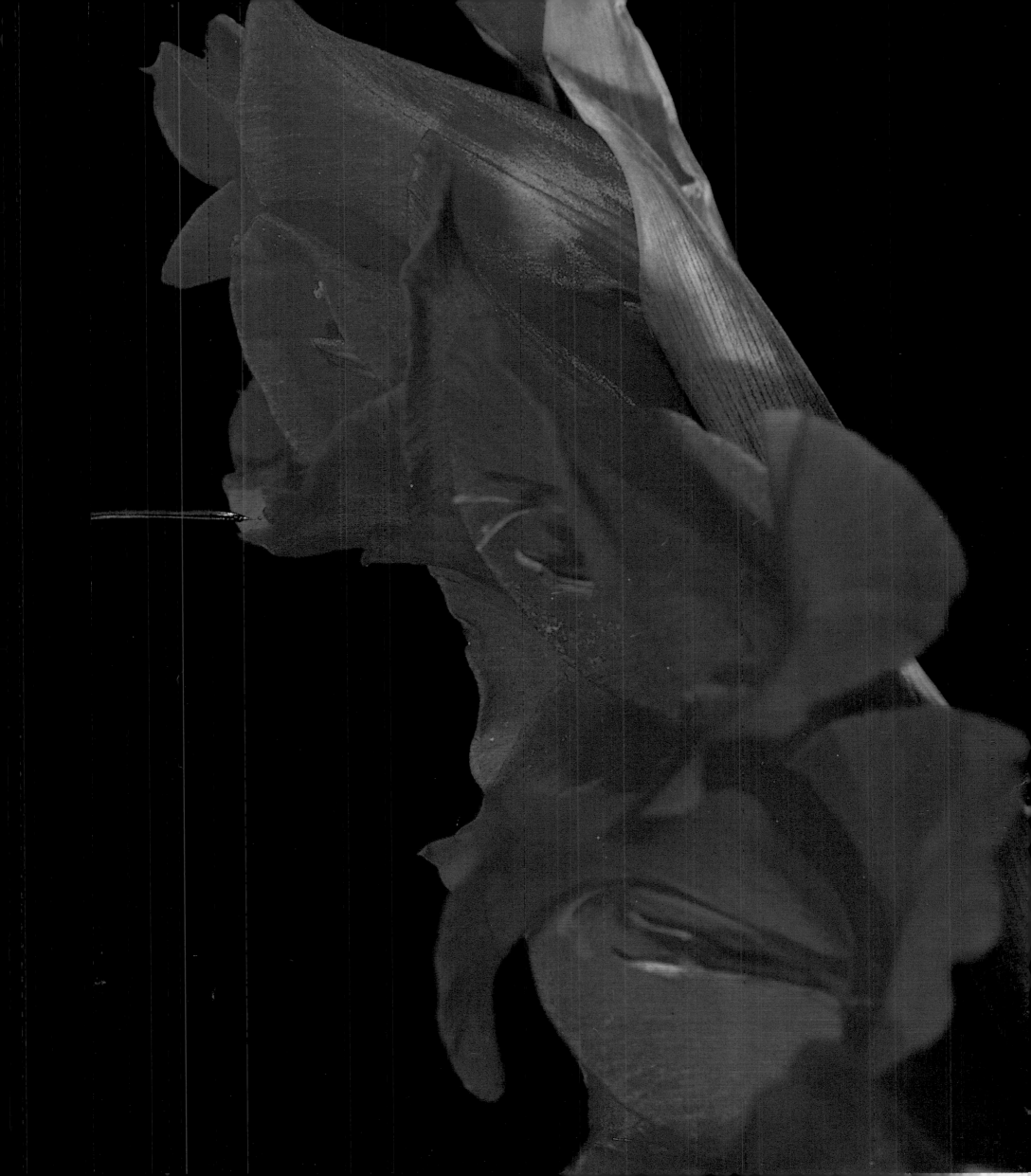

This page, top left: The female Anna's Hummingbird makes her nest in isolated locations far from areas occupied by other hummers. *Top right:* Two young Anna's Hummingbirds, just days from fledging, strain the capacity of their nest almost to breaking point. *Bottom left:* The somewhat dingy, grayish underparts of a female Anna's Humminbird, as well as its slightly larger body size, help to distinguish it from females of the very similar Costa's and Black-chinned Hummingbirds. *Bottom right:* Most North American hummingbirds are migratory, but the Anna's stays year-round in much of its range, although it is found in the Arizona desert and the mountains of Vancouver Island during winter. *Facing page:* A female Anna's Hummingbird perches at the edge of the nest. Built of plant down and spider's silk, the female often continues to build up the sides of the nest throughout incubation.

This page, top: With eyes situated on the side of its head, the hummingbird has a good range of vision.
This Anna's Hummingbird can keep watch for possible dangers while he feeds. *This page, bottom:* When
a hummer has found an abundant supply of food which will satisfy his daily energy requirements, he
will often perch himself on a high branch from which he can assess the area. *Facing page:* The adult male
Anna's Hummingbird has a rose-red helmet, a green back and a gray underside. During the molting
season, which lasts from late May until early September, these normally hostile and territorial birds manage
to live together in relative harmony.

Facing page: In the dry canyons of southern Arizona, New Mexico and west Texas lives the beautiful Broad-billed Hummingbird, feeding on the nectar of wildflowers that grow in this arid environment. *This page:* The female Broad-billed Hummingbird, as with most female hummers, is less colorful than her male counterpart. With her pale eyestripe, the female Broad-billed is sometimes confused with the rare White-eared Hummingbird.

Facing page: A male Broad-billed Hummingbird flies despite wide gaps in his wings where worn primary feathers have molted out. The missing feathers will be quickly replaced, however, as the new ones grow in.
This page: By beating its wings in a shallow, horizontal figure-eight, a hummingbird can hover in place, a feat no other bird can match. On average, a hummingbird's wings flap an astonishing 50 beats per second, and up to 200 per second in very fast flight.

Previous page: Just the tip of this male Broad-billed Hummingbird's tongue extends beyond the end of his bill, as he backs away from a scarlet penstemon. Scientists argued for years over how a hummingbird drinks, but high-speed photographs finally showed that nectar is taken onto the grooved tongue, then forced down the throat when the tongue is extended again. *Previous page, inset:* Leaning forward, a male Broad-billed Hummingbird drinks from the unusual, tubular flowers of the western coral bean, a shrub of the pea family that blooms in the early desert spring. *This page:* Green iridescence shimmers off the body feathers of this female Broad-billed, along with a subtle touch of blue on the edges of her tail. The Broad-billed Hummingbird has a peculiarly jerky flight, unlike the direct flight of most hummingbirds. *Facing page:* A female Broad-billed Hummingbird sips at a blooming cluster of ocotillo flower, a species of plant which is not pollinated by hummers, despite its popularity with the birds.

This page: A Broad-billed male perches among the spiky leaves of a yucca in southern Arizona. The species is restricted to a relatively small area in the Southwest, but ranges more widely in Mexico. *Facing page:* A stunning male Broad-billed Hummingbird, his blue tail flared and gorget shining, hovers above a blooming ocotillo in the Santa Rita Mountains of Arizona.

Previous page: Responding to the spring rains, an ocotillo bursts with flowers, the rich nectar of which makes it an attractive food plant for a number of hummingbird species. The plant gets nothing in return because it is pollinated not by hummingbirds, but by insects. *Previous page, inset:* The combination of a red-based bill and a rich, blue throat, mark this as a male Broad-billed Hummingbird. Young males, freshly fledged from the nest, may have a few blue flecks on the throat, but the full gorget does not develop until the following summer. *Facing page:* Caught in a shaft of sunlight, a Broad-billed Hummingbird pauses before feeding. Hummingbirds frequently seem tame around humans, but they are cautious when quick predators like Sharp-shinned Hawks are near. *This page:* Broad-billed Hummingbirds are one of several species that reach the northern edge of their range in the American Southwest, retreating into Mexico with the coming of winter.

This page: After bathing or feeding, the hummingbird will use his comblike claws to groom the feathers of the neck, head and throat. The bill is used to groom the remaining plumage. *Facing page, top and bottom:* Taking a moment of rest, a male Broad-billed Hummingbird perches on a slender twig. When nectar-bearing flowers are abundant, hummingbirds may feed for only 15 percent of the time, spending the remainder resting, preening or chasing rivals. Hummers have played a prominent role in ancient legends. One legend has it that Mexican warriors who died in battle were taken to the "mansion of the sun" where they were transformed into glittering hummingbirds.

Facing page: **Females of the Allen's Hummingbird, like this one, and the Rufous Hummingbird are virtually inseparable in the field, both having reddish sides and undertail coverts and a green back.** *This page:*
**Tail fanned, a female Allen's Hummingbird comes to a halt at a flower head which, with its tiny, tubular
blossoms, is perfectly suited to the bird's thin beak and long, probing tongue.**

Facing page: A common woodland species within its narrow range, the Allen's Hummingbird is found only in coastal California and the extreme south of Oregon. *This page:* The Latin genus name of the Allen's Hummingbird, *Selasphorus,* means "flame-bearing," a very apt description, as this male shows with his glowing orange-red gorget, green head and rust - colored body.

Previous pages: A lush meadow of wildflowers, bordering a woodland, provides a feast for hummingbirds. At the peak of blossoming, such a field may be alive with hummingbirds, butterflies and bees, all gorging on the nectar the flowers provide. *Left inset:* A belligerent Allen's Hummingbird, feathers fluffed in righteous anger, scans his territory for interlopers. This pugnacious species will not only chase other hummingbirds, but also Sharp-shinned Hawks and other predators as well. *Right inset:* It is hardly surprising that these beautiful feathers were once part of a lucrative business. Hummingbird skins were once sold for the production of ladies' feather fans and bonnets. *This page:* The Allen's Hummingbird is known for having one of the most elaborate courtship displays of any North American species; the male performs a series of diving pendulum swings, starting high in the sky and swooping down just over the female's head. *Facing page:* A female Allen's feeds her brood in the nest she built in a link of abandoned metal chain. A departure from the species' more usual nest sites on tree branches, but not unheard of for this bird.

This page: A paintbrush blossom lures a female Broad-tailed Hummingbird in for a drink. Paintbrushes are a diverse and widespread western group of flowers, and hummingbirds are important pollinators of most of them. *Facing page:* The tips of the outer primary feathers on each of the male Broad-tailed Hummingbird's wings are thin and slightly curved, producing a unique rattling trill in flight that serves as a handy identification tool for bird-watchers.

Previous pages: Prime Broad-tailed Hummingbird feeding habitat in the White Mountains of Arizona. Primarily a mountain species, the Broad-tailed is often found near flowing water and while it may feed in the open, it usually nests in coniferous woodlands. *Previous page, inset:* Common throughout the Rocky Mountains, the Broad-tailed Hummingbird follows a vertical progression in summer, as wildflowers bloom higher and higher in the melting alpine snows. *This page:* Her bark-flecked nest tucked beneath a conceal-ing branch, a female Calliope Hummingbird incubates her two eggs. Calliopes almost always build their nests in such protected locations, sheltered from the elements and danger. *Facing page:* This nestling was hatched from one of the smallest eggs in the avian world. They usually measure less than 1/2 an inch and weigh less than 1/2 a gram. Compare this to an ostrich egg which will average 6 1/2 inches long.

This page: Unlike other birds, young hummers do not acquire a downy coat. They have to rely totally on their mothers for warmth. Eight to twelve days after hatching they are able to maintain their own body temperatures. *Facing page:* Resting beside a pea-sized egg, a baby Calliope Hummingbird bristles with feather quills, which will soon erupt into the bird's juvenile plumage. Hummingbird eggs usually hatch at nearly the same time, so it is likely that the unhatched egg is infertile. *Overleaf:* With the snow-capped peaks of the Sierras in the background, alpine meadows bask in the summer light. The Calliope Hummingbird makes its home in the grasslands, wooded canyons and mountains of western North America and Mexico.

Facing page: The hummingbird has a reputation for skillful flying. It is capable of flying forwards, backwards, even upside down. Its unique skill is to hover motionless while feeding. *This page:* The smallest bird in North America, the Calliope Hummingbird weighs only three grams, and is just a fraction more than three inches long. This male shows the streaked, purple gorget that sets it apart from other North American hummingbirds.

These pages: Hummingbirds require great quantities of food because their weight-specific metabolic rates are extremely high. These Ruby-throated Hummingbirds will consume nectar for sugar and insects for protein. They also require water, most of which is supplied through nectar though sometimes they will drink from wet leaves.

This page: Elongated out of all proportion to the bird's size, the throat gorget of the male Costa's Hummingbird flares to either side like a metallic, purple mustache. Special cells on the surface of the gorget feathers split and modify sunlight, reinforcing the purple wavelengths and nullifying the others. *Facing page:* The long, arching spine of a cactus provides a convenient perch for a diminutive male Costa's Hummingbird, warming himself as the morning sun takes the night's chill out of the desert air. *Overleaf:* Cave Creek Canyon, in Arizona's Chiricahua Mountains, is home to as many as a dozen species of hummingbirds, including the rare Violet-crowned, Berylline and Lucifer hummers, and more common Black-chinned, Rufous and Broad-billed. *Inset, left:* The extrusile tongue and long narrow bill of the Costa's Hummingbird enables it to feed from tubular flowers like the Chuparosa. *Inset, right:* Patrolling his territory in the shadow of towering cactus, a Costa's Hummingbird will descend on intruders in a blistering aerial attack, borne on rapidly vibrating wings that whine, distressingly, like a passing bullet.

This page: Taking advantage of the bounty of the Sonora Desert, a Costa's Hummingbird probes for nectar. Ecologically, the deserts of the U.S. Southwest are merely an extension of Mexico, which explains the region's rich hummingbird life. *Facing page:* An inhabitant of the desert and chaparral, the Costa's Hummingbird arrives on its breeding grounds in March or April, but does not linger, usually retreating to its wintering grounds by late July. *Overleaf:* A sea of red flowers all but swallow a tiny Costa's Hummingbird, taking a midday meal on the wing. Many hummingbirds will defend such rich feeding areas from other hummers, as well as from large butterflies that would compete for nectar.

Facing page: The Costa Hummingbird's song differs from the rather unharmonious song of other species in that it ends with a distinctive , haunting whistle.*This page:* The Costa's Hummingbird migrates only short distances, unlike the Ruby-throated and Rufous who travel an amazing 2,000 miles or more. Surprisingly, this long journey is made in total solitude.

These pages: Attracted by a man-made feeder filled with sugar water, a Glittering Emerald brightens a garden in Bolivia. With its scalloped, green-edged body feathers, this species looks as though it were clad in medieval chainmail. By keeping the sweet liquid filled up, enthusiasts can create a haven for hummingbirds who will reward their benefactor with their loyalty to the territory.

This page: **An inhabitant of western Ecuador, the Violet-tailed Sylph is an eight-inch hummingbird of almost sublime beauty with a striking green back that blends, imperceptibly, into the cobalt blue of its long, forked tail.** *Facing page:* **The female Violet-tailed Sylph lacks the outlandishly long tail feathers of her mate, but her more subtle colors and short, forked tail make her an attractive creature nonetheless.**

Facing page: Most hummingbirds are born with 8 to 12 pairs of downy feathers. The Rufous-breasted
Hermit, like this one, is an exception, with 25 to 76 downy-type filaments at hatching. The plumage
appears soon afterwards. *This page:* The White-vented Plumeleteer is one of approximately 338 species and
116 genera of the family *Trochilidae*. Only the tyrant-flycatcher of the Americas
boasts a larger family.

Facing page: The Magnificent Hummingbird, which ranges through Mexico and much of Central America, enters the U.S. only in the extreme Southwest. Its range partially overlaps that of the ocotillo, on which this male is feeding. *This page:* As this female Magnificent Hummingbird clearly shows, a hummingbird's wing is little more than primary feathers, with rigid, fused bones beneath the leading edge to provide power and mobility, allowing it to hover and fly backwards.

This page: The Magnificent Hummingbird is rather common in the canyons and mountain meadows of extreme southern Arizona, Mexico and Texas and is one of the avian specialities that draws bird-watchers to that region each year. *Facing page:* The hummingbird spends so much of his life on the wing, that the process of evolution has rendered his feet useless for anything but sitting still on a twig.

Facing page: Showing the fickleness of iridescence, a male Magnificent Hummingbird shimmers with green on his breast and head, while his purple crown and green gorget show black. The result is a deceptively drab bird. *This page:* A droplet of ocotillo nectar glistens at the tip of this Magnificent Hummingbird's beak as he pauses in feeding. The Magnificent, at more than five inches, is the largest U.S. species, although still small when compared to most birds. *Overleaf:* His white underparts strikingly different from that of other North American male hummingbirds, a Violet-crowned hummer drinks at a feeder. Found only in the mountains of the Arizona-New Mexico border country, it is uncommon even there.

Facing page: The rapidly moving wings of this female Rufous Hummingbird leave a ghost-image, too fast for even the photographer's electronic flash. To the naked eye, the wings vanish in a blur, as though the hummingbird were supported by thin air. *This page:* The male Rufous Hummingbird is the only North American hummer with an all-orange back, sides and head; the closely related Allen's has a green back. The orange body feathers are pigmented rather than iridescent; consequently, the color can be seen regardless of the light direction.

Previous pages: Hurricane Ridge, Olympia is typical habitat of the Rufous Hummingbird. *This page:* Two Rufous Hummingbird chicks crowd their nest along Starr Creek in Oregon; the next day they fledged, taking to the air for the first time in their lives, three weeks after leaving the egg. *Facing page:* Like a shiny new penny brought to life, this male Rufous Hummingbird seems to be a feathered celebration of the color copper, except for the tiny flecks of iridescent green that flicker on the back of his wings.

This page: An immature Rufous Hummingbird points his beak to the sky, a clear warning for other males to stay away. The Rufous is one of the most pugnacious of hummers, eagerly taking on all unwanted visitors. *Facing page:* His throat flecked with the beginnings of a gorget but his back still green, this immature male Rufous Hummingbird will acquire the solid-orange back and copper throat of an adult before the next spring.

Previous pages: Yellow glacier lilies are one of the first flowers to bloom when the high country snows melt in Glacier National Park in Montana, providing early food for Rufous Hummingbirds. *Previous page, inset:* A single leaf can bear the minimal weight of this immature Rufous Hummingbird. *This page:* Minute insects, spiders and mites, caught in flight or gleaned from the blossoms of plants, are an important part of a hummingbird's diet. This male Rufous Hummingbird has captured a small bug. *Facing page:* An Indian paintbrush lures a Rufous Hummingbird to stop. The West's many species of paintbrushes are favorite hummingbird food plants and can be grown in wildflower gardens to attract hummers.

Facing page: A male Rufous Hummingbird perches on a creosote twig in the mountains near Tuscon, Arizona during the migration; this species breeds much farther north, from Wyoming and Oregon to Alaska, but passes through the Southwest en route from Central America. *This page:* Breathing life into a garden in Victoria, British Columbia, a male Rufous Hummingbird hovers before a flower. Rufous Hummingbirds range as far north as south-central Alaska, farther north than any other member of this tropical family.

This page: **This immature Blue-throated Hummingbird will share the drabness of his mother until his first prenuptial molt the following spring brings him the cerulean throat, green cap and white facial stripes of adulthood.** *Facing page:* **An ocotillo in the Chiricahua Mountains of Arizona tempts a male Blue-throated Hummingbird.** *Overleaf:* **A sequence of photographs shows how a male Blue-throated Hummingbird flaps on a horizontal plane to hover in front of a flower. The breastbone of a hummingbird has a very deep keel, to provide an anchor for the powerful chest muscles.**

Facing page: Back lighting rims a Blue-throated Hummingbird male beneath a blooming penstemon. By day, the hummingbird's heart rate may be 1,200 beats per minute, but to save energy at night the bird falls into a torpor, and the heartbeat drops to 36 per minute. *This page:* The rounded tail with large white spots is diagnostic of the male Blue-throated Hummingbird, the only North American species in which the male sports such eye-catching white patches. *Overleaf:* A stream flows beneath rocky cliffs in the southeast Arizona mountains, providing a cool oasis from the deserts that make up much of the state. This is perfect habitat for the uncommon Blue-throated Hummingbird.

This page: Almost hidden in the greenery of a remote canyon, a female Blue-throated Hummingbird incubates her two eggs in the confines of her tiny nest. Blue-throats usually pick a forked twig or a clump of wildflowers or ferns to support the nest. *Facing page:* The Blue-throated Hummingbird is second only to the Magnificent Hummingbird as North America's largest; males usually measure about five inches, and fly with wingbeats much slower than those of smaller hummers.

These pages: Two South American species. Above, a Brazilian Bronze Hummingbird and on the right, a White-tipped Sicklebill, which is a highly specialized hummingbird. Here it uses its unlikely shaped beak to reach inside a heliconia flower, where other birds cannot feed. Such an adaption reduces competition.

Facing page: Copper-rumped Hummingbird. The sparkling plumage of hummers seems to be solely for ornamentation. The dazzling colors of the male play an important role in courtship. *This page:* It is quite obvious why this hummer has been named the Brown Violet-ear. The streak of violet resembles a single jewel, adorned almost as an afterthought.

Facing page: Sporting a forked tail that more than doubles his length, this male Red-tailed Comet is about 7 inches long; this lovely species is found in the Andes from northern Argentina up into Bolivia.
This page: The largest hummingbird in the world, the Giant Hummingbird of the Andes reaches a length of more than eight inches, but still weighs less than an ounce. This is because, like all hummingbirds, it consists more of feathers than flesh and bone.

Facing page: **Some names given to hummingbirds, such as this White-chested Emerald, clearly allude to their jewel-like colors. In zoos worldwide, the aviaries housing them are referred to as "jewel rooms."**
This page: **The Latin name** *Aglaeactis cupripennis* **does not conjure up such a glorious image as the name given to this pretty bird, the Shining Sunbeam.**

This page: A Ruby-topaz Hummingbird sits on her tiny nest. She fluffs out and separates her feathers so that the eggs are directly against her brood patch. They require a great deal of warmth, sometimes around 90°F. *Facing page:* The vivid color on the chest of this Blue-chinned Sapphire gleams as the sunlight catches it. The hummer, the sunlight and the observer all have to be in exactly the right position for this wonderful display to be appreciated.

Facing page: Having fed, a female Black-chinned Hummingbird backs away from the flower, preparing to return to her nest, where she will regurgitate part of her meal of nectar and small insects to feed her young. Male hummingbirds play no part in rearing the chicks. *This page:* The female Black-chinned Humming-bird, shown here in a garden in Arizona, is indistinguishable from the female Ruby-throated Hummingbird of the East, causing confusion where the two species' ranges overlap in Texas.

This page: This Black-chinned Hummingbird appears to be motionless, caught suspended by the photographer's camera. To the naked eye the wings are barely distinguishable, just a blur as they work to keep within reach of the nectar. *Facing page:* The female Black-chinned Hummingbird is often mistaken for the female Anna's or Costa's. It does in fact differ from the Costa's in the degree of green in her tail and is smaller than the Anna's. *Overleaf:* A male Black-chinned Hummingbird waits while a female of the same species drinks. This is uncharacteristically peaceful behavior for a hummingbird, even between those of opposite sexes.

This page: The power of a back-stroke bends the wing feathers of this male Black-chinned Hummingbird. Only the lower third of the male's gorget is iridescent; the rest is truly black, no matter how the light strikes it. *Facing page:* When the light is right, the throat gorget of the Black-chinned Hummingbird flares into vivid violet, but only along the lower edges. It is the only North American species with such a two-toned throat. Here he hovers over a coral bean in Arizona. *Overleaf:* Wildflowers, blooming near the lip of a canyon, indicate the proper habitat for Black-chinned Hummingbirds, which are usually associated with semi-arid country across the West. *Overleaf, inset:* Although female hummingbirds usually raise one brood of chicks at a time, Black-chinned Hummingbirds, like this one, have been observed caring for two nests simultaneously.